D0122453

This Belongs To:

donna
brown Guillaume

You Got to Dance
with Them
What Brung You

MOLLY IVINS

You Got to Dance with Them What Brung You

★ POLITICS IN THE CLINTON YEARS ★

RANDOM HOUSE ★ NEW YORK

The articles that appear in this work were originally published in the
*Fort Worth Star-Telegram, Mother Jones, The Nation, The New York Times Book Review,
The New York Times Magazine,* and *The Progressive.*

Grateful acknowledgment is made to the following for permission to
reprint previously published material:

FAIR: Excerpt from *The Way Things Aren't: Rush Limbaugh's Reign of Error*
by Steven Rendall, Jim Noureckas, and Jeff Cohen. Copyright © 1995 by FAIR.
Reprinted by permission.

The Nation: Excerpt from "Conscience and Taxation" by Katha Pollitt
from the June 27, 1994, issue of *The Nation.* Reprinted with permission
from *The Nation* magazine.

The New York Times: Excerpt from "An Ageless Moliere Speaks to the Ages"
by David Richards (April 10, 1994). Copyright © 1994 by The New York Times
Company. Reprinted by permission.

Library of Congress Cataloging-in-Publication Data
Ivins, Molly.
You got to dance with them what brung you: politics in the Clinton years / Molly Ivins.
p.   cm.
ISBN 0-679-40446-5
1. United States—Politics and government—1993–   I. Title.
E885.I96   1998
973.929—dc21   97-35511

Random House website address: www.randomhouse.com
Printed in the United States of America on acid-free paper
24689753
First Edition

Book design by Jessica Shatan

This book is dedicated to the memory of

Ida and Jesse Frankel—
such wonderful people—

and to

the indispensable Elizabeth Peake Faulk.
As members of the Lizzie Fan Club nationwide know,
she's pretty fabulous folks her own self,
but you should never leave her on hold for long.

★ Acknowledgments ★

My favorite part again, where I get to recognize all the people who keep me going, 'cause Lord knows I couldn't do it by myself. For this book in particular, I am indebted to those who styled themselves "Team Molly" and who did all the grunt work: Jan Reid, the best writer ever fired by the idiots at *Texas Monthly;* Pat Booker, a consummate pro at the rapidly disappearing craft of real editing; and Mike Smith, the shy researcher and computer genius whose solid sense of values and emerging self-confidence ("Mike, call the White House!" "Who, me?") are a constant source of delight.

And, of course, the captain of the team, Liz Faulk, the linchpin of the whole deal, who has coached me through everything from the training of Athena-the-too-tall-poodle to the death of my mother. Some debts can never be repaid. But I am truly *fromaged*-off over this talk of retirement. When pigs fly!

Thanks to Hope Reyna ("There's Hope!") for keeping the home fires burning, not to mention the air-conditioning in working order. The Austin pals are especially dear: Sheila Cheaney, 1956 National Junior Baton Twirling Champion; Marilyn Schultz, broadcast journalism's gift to UT; and Courtney Anderson, artist and ditz extraordinaire.

My brother, Andy Ivins, his wife, Carla, and Dax, Drew, and Darby are dear to me beyond measure. Doesn't get better than Farkle Family Fun in Boerne, Texas. (This is especially for Drew, who has been waiting to be Acknowledged for a long damn time.)

The beloved *Fort Worth Star-Telegram* has changed hands three times since I joined it in 1990 and has been through more ups and downs than any newspaper should endure. It remains its own practical, quotidian self, stubbornly refusing to develop grandiose ambitions (no "*New York Times* of the Southwest" at our shop), but you still can't beat it for coverage of Cowtown and the mid-cities. Some may yearn to be associated with more prestigious journals, but I've been there, done that. I'll take the Startlegram's honest, down-home, no-bull approach any day (always excepting the time executive editor Jack Tinsley addressed the box on the wall under the impression it was a cost-reducing tape recorder; next day, a sign appeared on every box like that in the building that said, "Don't talk to me, I'm just a thermostat."). A long time ago editor Mike Blackman rode his Harley down to see me about a job: we shook hands on the deal. Many a time since then I've been asked, "No contract? No lawyers?" Nah. It's Fort Worth. That's the way we do things.

As usual, I keep writing for lefty editors who pay in the high two figures. Was there ever an easier gig than being back-page humor columnist for *The Progressive*? Get through that magazine, and anything will strike you funny. The beloved Erwin Knoll, God bless him (actually, I'm not sure Erwin believed in God, but what the hell, it can't hurt), went and croaked on us, but Matt Rothschild carries on nobly. Some suspect Rothschild of gradually making *The Progressive* more fun to read. Everything's relative.

My favorite gig of recent years was teaching at Cal-Berkeley's School of Journalism, courtesy of Doug Foster, associate dean of student affairs, which meant we had to have a lot of students screwing each other so Doug could keep his job (just a joke). Foster and Orville

Schell, the dean there and a semifamous journalist his own self, are putting together a terrific program. A hint here to aging journalists: Teaching is fabulous fun. The best. Of course, it does force you to figure out what you've been doing and why you've been doing it all these years. That can prove an interesting surprise.

I close with a thousand thanks—hell, a million—not only to those who have so generously helped me, but also to the politicians of America, who not only held still but also said "Cheese" for these snapshots.

✦Contents✦

WE THE PEOPLE

NOTES FROM THE REVOLUTION

★Introduction★

"Write about the Clinton years," they said.

"Find themes," they said.

So I suggested we call the book *Nausea*, but they said it wouldn't sell.

Publishers are difficult people.

In politics, it's better to be lucky than smart, and until recently, Bill Clinton seemed to be both. We Texans say of a lucky man, "They tried to hang him, but the rope broke." For six years now, Clinton's enemies have been trying to string him up with shoelaces that keep breaking on them. The scenario has taken on a delirious, almost ritual quality—like watching *The Perils of Pauline* as slapstick. Clinton does something to upset the R's, like firing the people in the White House travel office; they solemnly declare it's worse than Watergate, and then respond by appointing Al D'Amato to investigate his ethics, or Dan Burton to investigate anything.

Then the Republicans went out and got a good stout noose—campaign financing—but every time they pulled on it, it tightened around their own throats, too. Now they have him by the zipper, that ol' Devil sex. As I write this, the media are in a frenzy worthy of the Dead Diana. Clinton may have finally done himself in, but in such a fashion that no one can take any satisfaction from it. In this perfect symphony of People Behaving Badly—from Clinton to Ms. Lewinsky to Ms. Tripp to Ken Starr—there is no redeeming social value. If he stays, he is politically crippled. If he goes, no one will be able to say, "The system worked." That our system for nailing politicians needs fixing is the clearest lesson to emerge so far from the Lewinsky affair.

Clinton himself remains a curiously opaque figure, our national Rorschach test. There is about Clinton a touch of Chauncey Gardiner, the figure in the film *Being There* into whom one could read whatever one liked. That he is regularly denounced by extreme right-wing propagandists as a multiple murderer, drug dealer, and perpetrator of other heinous crimes is in jarring juxtaposition to the more common perception that he is spineless, gutless, and unwilling to fight. If he's really a wimp, how come he inspires such virulent hatred?

I have wasted more time and space defending Clinton than I care to think about. If left to my own devices, I'd spend all my time pointing out that he's weaker than bus-station chili. But the man is so constantly subjected to such hideous and unfair abuse that I wind up standing up for him on the general principle that some fairness should be applied.

In looking at the anti-Clinton sentiment sloshing around the country, one first has to separate out the well-financed propaganda machine funded largely by Richard Mellon Scaife of Pittsburgh. We have not previously seen anything like this deliberate attempt to ruin a president. Scaife is reportedly obsessed with conspiracy theories and is the chief financial backer of the virtual industry dedicated to inventing and purveying the most far-fetched and outlandish tales about Clinton.

But even if one sets aside the Scaife-backed propaganda, Clinton does inspire a distinctly odd strain of hatred. It is curiously reminiscent of the hatred incurred by John F. Kennedy. Before Kennedy became "the martyred president," officially mourned by one and all, there was a wiggy kind of Kennedy hatred familiar to anyone who spent time around Dallas in the early 1960s. Some of it came from the John Birch Society, but even more was touched off by class resentment, an intense envy of someone who was rich and handsome and seemed always to have had it easy. And much as I hate to dabble in armchair psychoanalysis, honesty compels me to recall that a great deal of it was also about S-E-X.

When you listen to the Clinton-haters, either on talk radio, in bars, or in their delightful correspondence, you notice that same not-very-subliminal resentment of someone who seems to be getting a lot. Clinton is not a manly man—he's no John Wayne—and is clearly in touch with his feminine side, as they say in pop psychology. That too touches off some kind of rage with at least a portion of the populace. I have no expertise on American sexual hang-ups, I don't know what it means, I just know it's there.

What in Kennedy's case was class resentment in Clinton's case is generational resentment. That Clinton, who was always the very model of an ambitious young pol, should have come to stand in many minds for the largely mythical sixties generation of longhaired, dope-smoking, draft-dodging, sex-crazed hippies is just one more example of the excess of irony in our time. It's also amazing that those resentments still persist so vividly after thirty-five years, but those who recall the anger of anti-anti-war protesters in those years will remember that there was a fair component of both class resentment and sexual envy involved at the time. In addition, Clinton is the subject of much continuing unfavorable comment from fellow baby boomers who don't seem to care much for their own cohort. The Washington press corps is rife with them. I envision a new course of therapy appearing any day now: help for self-hating boomers.

Another factor is a theory devoutly believed by many black citizens in this country: that "they" are out to get Bill Clinton because he cares about and champions black people. I'm not vouching for this theory; I'm just reporting that many black people believe it. Each of us is different with different people: some bring out the best in us, others the worst. It is observably true of Bill Clinton that he is at his best on the subject of race in front of a black audience. He is genuine and comfortable. The best speech I ever heard him make, and one of the best I ever heard about race in this country, was in Texas on the day of the Million Man March in D.C. It got almost no public attention: the media were too busy reporting the bizarre maunderings of Louis Farrakhan. But you could look it up.

Still another strain of baseless attack on Clinton, also common in the D.C. press corps, is that he must be a hick because he's from Arkansas, which in turn must be Dogpatch. Max Frankel of *The New York Times* once explained during a television interview why the *Times* felt it had to send reporters down to reinvestigate the Whitewater story. "Clinton," said Frankel, with the splendid provincialism only a New Yorker can manage, "came from *nowhere.*" Clinton had been governor of Arkansas for ten years at that point. And believe it or not, the Arkansas press is perfectly capable of adequately investigating a minor-league land deal. (For a delightful rundown of this brand of snobbery, see Gene Lyons's book *Fools for Scandal.*)

As a Texan who went to an Ivy League school myself, I do understand Clinton in this regard. He is neither ambivalent about his dual cultural heritage, nor does it make him a fake in either milieu. It's like being able to speak two languages: if you can, you can; it doesn't mean there's anything phony about you.

Yet another common conclusion about Clinton is that the man is a moral dwarf. This could be. I barely know him personally and have seen no symptoms of sainthood by observing him from afar. But then the question arises concerning those who make the claim: Which of them has, as it were, standing to sue in this regard? Frankly, Newt Gingrich doesn't strike me as a likely plaintiff. Nor do my colleagues in the political press corps, whom I know rather better than I do Mr. Clinton. The man has always struck me as a politician, a breed for which I have some residual fondness. What were they expecting, Ajax by way of Aristotle?

That none of this has much to do with Clinton's performance as president is part of the problem of dealing with the man fairly. It all swirls around him in great clouds of obfuscation, preventing anyone from getting a clear take on what kind of a job the man has done.

We know a few things about Clinton after all this time: He's a genuine policy wonk, he works hard, and he is almost invariably polite. We know Clinton has a temper—when he found out one of his aides had been using a government helicopter to ferry himself to the golf course, Clinton got so mad he busted up a substantial chair. But in his six years as president, we have seen him display only the mildest irritation in public on two occasions. And given the amount of abuse he has taken, I call that a remarkable record. Were his momma alive, I would write to congratulate her—she taught that boy manners. Nor does he whine in public. He has been gracious and forgiving toward any number of people who have said astonishingly distasteful things about him—David Brinkley, Newt Gingrich, and Trent Lott come to mind. A common strain of Clinton criticism is that the man has no control of his appetites, either for sex or food, and the Lewinsky case and related matters may yet prove this to be true. Yet based on the public record, one would have to say he shows a remarkable degree of self-mastery.

Clinton has been attacked for dropping his friends when they're in trouble; he has been attacked for helping his friends when they're in trouble; he has been attacked for withholding information when accused of something; he has been attacked for dumping great loads of it; he has been attacked for taking responsibility for disaster (as after the '94 election) and for failing to take responsibility (most of the rest of the time). Again, I'm damned if I want to get stuck with the defense brief for this guy, but doesn't this strike anyone else as just a trifle unfair?

The Republicans have a new ploy with Clinton: Whenever they do something particularly stupid—like shutting down the government or failing to send disaster relief to flood victims in the upper Midwest—their response to looking like idiots is to announce solemnly that Bill Clinton is a *great* politician. A backhanded compliment if ever there was one.

Actually, he's not. If his adversaries weren't so inept, he'd look a lot worse than he does. Clinton told me in '92 that he thought he was the right president for the times because he knew how to deal with Republicans. He meant those Rockefeller (Winthrop, that is) Republicans they have in Arkansas; he'd never seen anything like the Shiite Republicans who came to dominate Congress in '94. One of his problems as president is that he spent too long as governor of Arkansas. What all Southern states have in common is the weak-governor system. It's a hangover from Reconstruction: having had Yankee governors forced upon us, we were determined never to let anything like that happen again and all wrote constitutions giving the governor practically no power. As a consequence, Clinton learned to deal for everything he wanted: Here's a piece for you, Sam; George, you'll like this part; Mary, I fixed that section you didn't like. Clinton plays politics in D.C. the same way he did in Arkansas—gives away nine tenths of the loaf just to get one slice. And he still hasn't figured out he doesn't have to do it. Not a clue how to play hardball.

The R's and the special interests ate him alive on health-care reform, even when he had a Democratic majority. Were it not for their egregious overreaching, he'd have nothing in the win column now. I point out, with some provincial pride, that my state has done more than its share to make Clinton look good: we sent Dick Armey, Tom DeLay, and Bill Archer up to Washington. You'd have to have the IQ of a dust bunny not to make points with foils like those.

Then comes the larger question: Even if Clinton knew how to play hardball, would he? The enigma of the man is whether or not he holds a belief for which he would be willing to do battle. No one but a fool or a Republican ever took him for a liberal: he's a DLC Democrat, the Democratic Leadership Council being the outfit that decided years ago that the most important task facing the Democratic party was to eradicate its reputation for taxing and spending. A shrewd strategy politically, but it doesn't have much to do with human betterment. Or justice.

While many of my fellow liberals washed their hands of Clinton years ago, as a longtime student of the Texas legislature, where progress comes only in the smallest of increments, I stayed with him until the summer of 1996. That's when he signed the welfare "reform" bill. My expectations of Democratic politicians exceed my expectations of Republicans by only the smallest of margins; but real Democrats don't hurt children. Clinton did.

When in doubt, the physicians' motto "Do No Harm" is not a bad one, but this "reform" is not a wash. Welfare "*de*form" will do terrible damage to children, and no one can pretend it could not be seen coming. One thing civilians—those who are not professionally involved in politics one way or another—fail to grasp is that political decisions are rarely between right and wrong. The main reason decisions become "issues" is because they're tough. You get a lot of 51–49 calls in politics, which is one reason I so despise certitude. Show me a politician given to self-doubt, and I'll show you one I respect. But welfare deform was not 51–49. The lives of one million children do not make a close call.

By way of less-than-refreshing contrast to Clinton, we have also been enjoying the First Republican Congress in Forty Years, led by the ineffable Newt Gingrich. And what a sight it was to see all our public scolds, who cannot abide Clinton's moral imperfections, take up the cry that Gingrich was a man of destiny. Lest we forget how the Speaker bestrode the political world like a colossus, his every zany pronouncement greeted with reverent awe in those early days of the Republican revolution, I recommend a short course in rereading the insane puffery of the time. Aside from the singular nastiness of his political rhetoric, which is both vicious and vulgar, Gingrich is a profoundly silly man. Deep down, he's shallow. As a political and social philosopher, he has advocated everything from orphanages to space travel for the populace without official Washington noticing that he's a fool.

I have come to believe Gingrich suffers from a form of Tourette's syndrome—he cannot stop himself from periodically lashing out with a teeth-rattling meanness of spirit despite his repeated vows to take up statesmanship. Actually, he's a lot less entertaining in his states-man mode, besides which, it seems to incite his more bloodthirsty fel-low Republicans to dump him. The inexpressibly goofy trio of Texans—Armey, DeLay, and Archer—stand behind him like Huey, Dewey, and Louie, reminding us that things can always get worse.

One must admit, the Republican Congress has a certain antic charm. Many of them are apparently genuinely convinced that gov-ernment is Evil. "Vote for me, I'm against government" seems an un-likely slogan, but there it is. Having come to the capital to "change the way Washington works," they proceeded to make it worse. Allow-ing lobbyists to rewrite regulatory laws, attempting to dismantle the Environmental Protection Agency, and collecting boatloads of corpo-rate campaign contributions in return is not a fresh beginning. Shut-ting it down wasn't much of an idea either, was it? Nor is privatizing the whole damn thing. Hiring Fly-by-Nite Garbage to take care of nuclear waste will not, one forebodes, work out well in the long run.

Personally, I think government is a tool, like a hammer. You can use a hammer to build or you can use a hammer to destroy; there is nothing intrinsically good or evil about the hammer itself. It is the purposes to which it is put and the skill with which it is used that de-termine whether the hammer's work is good or bad. If hammers were cussed as often and as vigorously as government, no doubt some Tim McVeigh would have parked a loaded Ryder truck outside a hammer factory by now. Cussing government in a democracy is a peculiar thing to do: it is, after all, us.

There is a still larger context in which to review the Clinton years: Our political system has been thoroughly corrupted, and by the usual suspect—money, what else? The corruption is open, obscene, and un-mistakable. The way campaigns are financed is a system of legalized bribery. We have a government of special interests, by special inter-ests, and for special interests. And that will not change until we change the way campaigns are financed.

That is the real, and indeed the only, theme of this book. "You got to dance with them what brung you" is one of the oldest sayings in politics. There's all kinds of special-interest money in politics. There's your National Rifle Association, your Women's Political Caucus, your Left-Handed Piccolo Players—not an organized group in America that doesn't have a PAC these days. But when you look at political money in the aggregate, more than 60 percent of it, almost two thirds, comes from organized corporate special interests. And they get what they pay for. Except that the rest of us wind up paying for it eventually. Corporate welfare, tax breaks, subsidies, loopholes: it's breathtaking, it's astonishing. The shift in the burden of taxation from corporations to individual taxpayers is stunning, and the shift from wealthy individuals to those who are the losers in an increasingly two-tiered economy is almost as striking. The story is underreported but still well understood. The playing field tilts more all the time. And the people know it.

As a card-carrying small-d democrat, I find the level of hatred for government both sad and dangerous. We are far beyond the cheerful cynicism of Mr. Dooley: people loathe politicians. I actually like politicians, a position so spectacularly unfashionable I've been wondering if I couldn't find some more socially acceptable perversion. Perhaps interspecies dating.

Our politicians have truly made a pact with the Devil. One watches them spend more and more of their time and energy grubbing, coaxing, flattering, and whoring for money. Terrified of being cut off from the mother's milk, they stand like morons in the rising sea of contempt that threatens to drown the whole system. Then they wonder why no one likes them anymore.

The economy of the Clinton years, a word always preceded by "booming," has produced definitive evidence that a rising tide does not lift all boats. No one repealed the laws of nature. We just had the wrong metaphor from the git-go. While the top two fifths of the people continue to get richer, the bottom three fifths barely hold on. All this has been examined and explained by folks more learned in the dismal science than I. But it is closely related to the decisions of those who govern us. And they got to dance with them what brung 'em.

The good news is that it's fixable. In fact, it's not that hard to fix. I'm too old to believe in simple solutions, but public campaign financing is the place to start. Before we do anything else, we need to get the government off the corporate payroll. Put your money, marbles, and chalk into that one.

This is a fairly gloomy report on the state of the Republic. I'm surprised by it myself. I have always enjoyed politics, both the complexities and strategies of the game and the vast, Dickensian comedy of it all. I am more angry than I had realized about how deeply the corruption of money has eaten into the soul of democracy. I recently ran a contest among my newspaper readers asking for suggestions for a campaign-finance reform slogan: roughly half the thousands of respondents used the words *whores* or *prostitution.* They are not mistaken.

This country is stuffed full of nice folks. You can meet 'em almost anywhere, even in Washington, D.C. It's not so much that we need to take up arms against a sea of troubles. We just need to get the hogs out of the creek so the water can clear up.

Molly Ivins
January 1998

Conscience of
a Liberal

What We Have Here Is a Failure to Be Kind

One Hundred Days.

Item: Senator Alfonse D'Amato goes on radio to crudely mock Lance Ito, the judge in the O. J. Simpson trial, by using an "Ah-so" kind of Oriental accent to imitate Ito, a third-generation American who has no accent.

Item: Senator Jesse Helms, chairman of the Senate Foreign Relations Committee, introduces Benazir Bhutto, the female prime minister of Pakistan, as the prime minister of India. Not once, but twice. Pakistan and India are deadly enemies.

Item: Howard Stern, a shock-radio host, uses the occasion of the murder of an exceptionally beautiful and talented twenty-three-year-old woman, Selena Quintanilla Perez, not only to speak of her with ridicule and contempt but to sneer at the grief of Hispanics about her death and at them in general. "Alvin and the Chipmunks have more soul than Selena"; "Spanish people have the worst taste in music. They have no depth." Stern plays some of Selena's music with the sound of bullets in the background.

Item: Representative Dick Armey of Texas refers to Representative Barney Frank of Massachusetts as "Barney Fag."

Item: The mother of House Speaker Newt Gingrich tells Connie Chung that her son considers Hillary Clinton "a bitch."

Item: Representative Robert Dornan accuses President Clinton of treason for having opposed the war in Vietnam.

Item: Representative Gerald Solomon, new chairman of the House Rules Committee, puts up a portrait of a notorious racist and segregationist in the committee room until black lawmakers complain.

Item: Gingrich, defending himself against the same kind of ethical questions he once raised against former Speaker Jim Wright, says his case is different because Wright is "a crook." Jim Wright was never indicted—much less convicted—for anything.

Item: Gingrich says women "have biological problems staying in a ditch for thirty days because they get infections." This was followed by his equally surprising announcement that "men are biologically programmed to hunt giraffes."

Item: In New York, the Senate majority leader says Democrats opposing welfare reform are beholden to blacks and Hispanics, "the people that got their hands out."

Item: In Texas, state senator John Leedom, speaking to a group of Republican homosexuals, several times refers to them as "queers."

We have a problem here, folks.

I was raised in East Texas, I live in south Austin, and I'm not about to pretend that racism, sexism, and homophobia aren't common as dirt in this country. Any time I want to hear someone use ugly words, I don't even have to leave my neighborhood. But it has not been common to hear this kind of language in public debate in this country for years.

This has nothing to do with political correctness. This is as simple as manners. And as every good soul who ever tried to teach you good manners said, manners are just about kindness. About being a little thoughtful of others. It's just as simple as the Golden Rule: "Do unto others as you would have them do unto you."

4

I once would have said, before multiculturalism and Pat Robertson changed my outlook on life, that kindness is the simple expression of Christianity. Robertson reminds us that the old Christian sin of anti-Semitism still lives.

Now comes the question: Does this tenor in the change of our public debate reflect us? Yes, there is racism, sexism, and homophobia in the land, so are our leaders and talk-show hosts just finally starting to mirror what's out here? Or is this just a new wrinkle in an old cultural debate that you can see clearly as far back as the works of Mark Twain?

In Twain's books one finds the thesis that women and preachers are in an unholy alliance to prevent normal, fun-loving boys from getting dirty, spitting, fishing, drinking, using dirty words, and otherwise having a fine time. The aim of this unholy alliance was to force boys to wear stiff collars and sit in church getting their behinds bored off.

Because I always wanted to be one of the people floating down the river on a raft—spitting, fishing, drinking, cussing, and otherwise having a fine time—I have done my fair share of rebelling against gentility and boring preachers. But I never confused gentility with kindness. Neither did Twain's greatest character, the man called by the now politically incorrect name Nigger Jim. If our shock jocks and right-wing pols want to learn the difference between stifling gentility and real courage, real kindness, and real nobility, I suggest that they go back and study Jim.

Fort Worth Star-Telegram
April 13, 1995

We Shall Not Let Evil Cowards Make Us Less Free

Sometimes there is solace just in having the right words to use, in being able to call something exactly what it is. I would like to thank President Clinton for the phrase "evil cowards."

Evil cowards killed babies in the springtime. Evil cowards made death in Normal, Oklahoma. A pickup truck, they say. Of course: so normal in Oklahoma. The cop with the beer gut, so normal, with an expression of anguish on his plain face, rushing the dying baby to a fireman. All those voices—in agony, in shock, in rage—all with that twanging, normal Oklahoma accent.

Evil cowards.

My God, the pointlessness of it. Why? What for? Who in Oklahoma City has the power to change the world?

Power, say the shrinks. It gives the evil cowards a sense of power. Vulnerability, say the shrinks. The evil cowards want us to feel vulnerable. But what good does that do them?

Wars have been caused by terrorists. We've been in some. Remember the *Maine.* The assassination of the archduke in Sarajevo. But who would give the evil cowards the satisfaction of letting us get dragged into their conflicts? Even in the Middle East, they know better; they continue to make peace despite the evil cowards, and that takes real courage. Even in Ireland, they ignore the evil cowards.

Sometimes the evil cowards want to provoke reaction. The Baader-Meinhof gang rampaged through Germany in the 1970s, hoping to provoke a fascist reaction, hoping to show that liberal democracy could not survive terrorism. Even in Germany, they did not give in to the evil cowards that time.

The impulse to make ourselves safer by making ourselves less free is an old one, even here. When we are badly frightened, we think we can make ourselves safer by sacrificing some of our liberties. We did it during the McCarthy era out of fear of communism. Less liberty is regularly proposed as a solution to crime, to pornography, to illegal immigration, to abortion, to all kinds of threats. But we shall not let evil cowards make us less free.

Fanatics have always said, "Things have to get worse before they can get better." Such evil nonsense. And mothers have always replied, "Not with my child's life."

Fort Worth Star-Telegram
April 23, 1995

7

We're Talking About This
Kind of People . . .

"Who *are* these people?" Glad you asked. I'm in regular correspondence with them myself. Here's a billet-doux that arrived just last week:

"Molly Ivins: We have a strong response to leftist, feminazi, elitist media persons such as yourself. You are an enemy of the White race, the White family unit and White America. You will be defeated along with your agenda of social subversion and decay. The People of Cincinnati and of the Nation have rejected your agenda and your clown prince Clinton. We are taking our nation back and we are ready to deal with you and your ilk by any means necessary! WE DESPISE YOU AND YOUR KIND!!!"

Follows a small sticker in black, red, and white with a swastika and the slogan WHITE POWER! Also appended: a copy of a column I wrote with "Commie Fag Lover" scrawled across my picture and some uncharitable and unprintable suggestions on it. Just a regular piece of fan mail in the daily life of a leftist, feminazi, elitist media person like myself.

Except for the piercing logic of calling someone a "feminazi" in a letter with a swastika pasted on it for identification, this is pretty impressive.

This is one of the less loony pieces of White Power mail I receive. The ones about the supposed invasion of this country by the United Nations are truly far gone in paranoia, not to mention the remarkable theory that President Clinton is about to import 100,000 Chinese cops to take people's guns away.

O.K., so we more or less know who these people are, but what's *wrong* with them? Why would they so completely suspend disbelief as to fall for this stuff? Who in his right mind could believe any of this? Twenty-five years in the newspaper bidness have given me a fairly strong faith in the proposition that if you haven't read about it in *The Daily Disappointment* or seen it on the network news, it's probably not true.

Oddly enough, I happen to agree with the White Power nuts on both the Branch Davidian case and the Randy Weaver case—gross misuses of government power, as I said at the time. But don't let them con you into thinking that the bombing in Oklahoma City is somehow the government's fault. These same cuckoo birds have been dinging around in the ozone about the Bureau of Alcohol, Tobacco and Firearms (known in their literature as *BATFAG*) for years and years now. It should also be pointed out that BATF's famous forensic lab cracked the World Trade Center bombing case and will probably provide the evidence in the Oklahoma case.

White Power, the KKK, the Lone Star Militia (and related branches) are all part of the same old racist, hate-mongering bunch of cockroaches who have been around all our lives. These belly-creeping dimwits are haters, which gets us into the same old trap: What do you do about hating the haters?

The phenomenal torrent of rhetoric unleashed by the Republican right lately on the theme that Government Is the Enemy plays right into the hands of the haters. The more people talk about government as Them, some unreachable, uncontrollable Other, the more extreme the haters get. I've got news for the haters: Government Is Us in this country. Well, us and a lot of corporate special-interest money. (Speaking of corporate special-interest money, perhaps the timber, mining, and ranching interests would now like to rethink their funding of the increasingly violent antienvironmental groups.)

Does this mean anyone who criticizes the gummint should now shut up, lest we somehow encourage the scum who are willing to kill children in their blind hatred? Of course not. But as I have been preaching for a long time: Listen to the people who are talking about how to fix what's wrong, not the ones who just work people into a snit over the problems. Listen to the people who have ideas about how to fix things, not the ones who just blame others.

Do I think the climate of hate speech, hate radio, and hate politics contributed to the torn, tiny bodies in Oklahoma City? I know they did. The poisoning of the well of public debate by people like Representative Bob Dornan, now running for the presidency of the United States, is just as much a part of the bomb that went off in Oklahoma as the fertilizer that went into it. Hate speech *is* fertilizer for bombs.

So should we limit freedom of speech? Of course not. But with freedom comes responsibility, and people should be held accountable for their words. And the rest of us have a responsibility, too: to use our own freedom to speak out against the haters.

The poisonous stew of gun nuts, racists, right-wingers, and religious zealots has been allowed to boil and bubble, heated by paranoia and lies, until it finally exploded. And it turned out that all the macho fantasies of all the losers who like to play at war were just the miasma of sick minds—there was no enemy. There were only mothers, fathers, sons, daughters, sisters, brothers, husbands, and wives. And babies.

Fort Worth Star-Telegram
April 25, 1995

Folks Aren't Really Good at Heart? I'm Not Giving Up

The municipal motto of Northfield, Minnesota, is "Cows, Colleges and Contentment." Honest. Last year they had a contest to think up a new motto and, after some civic thought, decided to keep "Cows, Colleges and Contentment."

So as we veer rhetorically toward the apocalypse as various social prophets mutter direly about the growth of the underclass, the unraveling of the social fabric, the brutalization of consciousness, and other pesky problems, you'll be happy to know that somewhere the sun is shining, somewhere the skies are bright, somewhere the children are laughing, et cetera. In Northfield, Minnesota, for one.

Having just survived a heavy dose of apocalyptic rhetoric the other night in New York City, I was especially glad to land where all the children are above average. Not that Minnesota is problem-free: on the front page of Friday's Minneapolis *Star Tribune,* we find enumerated three certifiable cases in which the Monied Special Interests have triumphed over the Will of the People in Minnesota in recent years. Three, count 'em—on the fingers of one hand.

The proximate cause of the current bout of apocalyptic analysis is that this year is the fiftieth anniversary of practically everything. As such, it's a handy vantage point for surveying as depressing a half-century of history as recorded time can offer. The last half of the twentieth century is never going to rank as a humanist high point; the fact that it was supposed to be the American Century is only further cause for depression.

It started with a Holocaust. Have you heard the interviews with the soldiers who first liberated Dachau? And it is ending with two more, Rwanda and Bosnia, about which no one is doing much of anything. In between, we've spent fifty years in denial about Hiroshima and Nagasaki, managed to get involved in a ten-year war we now acknowledge was "terribly wrong," and built enough nuclear weapons to blow up the earth and everyone on it several times over. We can't even sit around and gloat about the Soviets because they've disbanded themselves.

If it weren't for the automatic teller machine and the self-cleaning garlic press, we'd have no evidence of progress at all—and I know people who think ATM's are part of a plot to prevent people from getting to know one another.

As an inveterate optimist, I hate arguing optimism versus pessimism, especially with people who are well informed. Let's face it: The evidence is always on the side of the pessimists. In fact, one of the few pro-optimism arguments that works is to point out that things can always get worse, which means we should be cheerful right now, because now will eventually turn out to be the Good Old Days.

Going onto a college campus these days—or even facing a junior-high audience for that matter—involves some tricky juggling. Telling kids to go forth and change the world may not be fair. On the other hand, telling them they're bound to have a hard time and shouldn't get their hopes up is not a peppy message.

Katha Pollitt, the feminist sage, observes that it's rather a shame that Americans have had to shed so many illusions during the last fifty years, mostly illusions about our own innocence and power. But she believes that it's a shame in the same sense that it's a shame that smoking causes cancer. It's too bad, but there it is. Are we not better off without illusions? Better off facing the very real limits on our national power and, certainly, the limits on our national innocence?

I suspect she's right; she often is. But I don't believe that recognizing the evil we have done in the course of our endless efforts to maintain our good opinion of ourselves means we must dislike ourselves. Rather an alarming number of Americans already don't like their fellow Americans—with good cause, they would all maintain. We seem to have gone from the old stereotype of Americans as fat, dumb, and happy to a new stereotype of fat, dumb, and unhappy.

After the bleak consideration of the last fifty years at the New York colloquium, one member of the audience was so depressed that she stood up and read Anne Frank's beautiful statement that ends, "I still believe that people are really good at heart."

"So look what happened to Anne Frank" is the obvious response. God bless the child, but her death is enough to make anyone doubt that people are really good at heart. There is a kind of bitterness that one finds among Holocaust survivors that is unanswerable. One of them, interviewed in the documentary *Shoah* and asked what was in his heart, said: "If you could open my breast and lick my heart, you would be poisoned and die from the bitterness of it."

They are entitled to their bitterness. The rest of us are not.

Fort Worth Star-Telegram
May 7, 1995

In McVeigh's Case, Going by the Book Was a Bad Idea

Beware the man who has read only one book.

— SOME DISTINGUISHED OLD ROMAN

Time magazine, which was granted an interview with Tim McVeigh's father and sister, is puzzled: "How Timothy McVeigh, coming from this background, could have evolved into an embittered right-wing loner, drifter and government hater is not easy to imagine." *Time* doesn't mention it, but according to McVeigh's friends, the answer seems to be that he became obsessed with a book: *The Turner Diaries* by Andrew Macdonald.

Normally when you meet someone obsessed with a book, it's the Bible. David Koresh, for example. Or in the case of Muslims, the Koran.

Some fundamentalists, who believe in biblical inerrancy, still refer all questions to the authority of the Good Book, undeterred by the fact that the Bible contradicts itself here and there. When I visited the Soviet Union many years ago, I met people given to settling all questions by referring to the works of V. I. Lenin, whose work is a lot more contradictory than the Bible and not nearly as well written.

Sometimes in Libertarian circles, one finds people obsessed with Ayn Rand, a twentieth-century popularizer of a sort of mutant nineteenth-century social science taken from Darwin: Life is a jungle, and only the strong survive.

Because *The Turner Diaries* has now played such a bizarre role in our life as a nation, I set out to read it. It's published by National Vanguard Books in Hillsboro, West Virginia, is not found in most bookstores, and has to be sent for. McVeigh carried copies with him as he traveled around the country and pushed them on other people at gun shows.

The book is made up of the fictional jottings of one Earl Turner, American White Man, as he takes part in a war between the "Patriots" and the U.S. government between 1991 and 1993. Turner is a member of a small, revolutionary band called the Order, and the immediate cause of the rebellion against the government is that the government has tried to take away people's guns. Members of the Order hide theirs instead. In a wonderfully loopy touch, members of Human Relations Councils come around and search for them.

But the larger issue in *The Turner Diaries* is race; it is quite simply a racist fantasy in which Patriots are people who understand that the white race is superior and that blacks and Jews must be killed. Anyone who doesn't agree is a liberal who must also be killed. The point at which the country started going wrong was its fight against the Nazis in World War II; we should have supported Adolf Hitler, according to the *Diaries,* and now it is up to the few in the Order to save the white race.

Early in the book, the Order blows up FBI headquarters with a truck bomb. The recipe for what destroyed the Murrah Federal Building in Oklahoma City, if you are interested, is on pages 35–36. In fact, one of the few interesting aspects of this book is the amount of technical detail it provides for everything from how to illegally tap into electrical power to the best way to blow up a nuclear power plant. In this regard, the book has the same fascination as a Tom Clancy techno-thriller—ah, so that's how that works!

After reading the entire book about how the Order saved white America, I'm left with one question: Why bother? In Macdonald's fantasy, white Americans are such a sorry bunch that it's hard to imagine why anyone would want to save them from anything. A random sampler: "Americans have lost their right to be free . . . slavery is the just and proper state for a people who have grown as soft, self-indulgent, careless and credulous and befuddled as we have. Indeed, we are already slaves. We have allowed a diabolically clever, alien minority [Jews] to put chains on our souls and our minds."

Turner, I regret to report, is given to philosophical musings: "Can we justly blame what has happened to us entirely on deliberate subversion, carried out through the insidious propaganda of the controlled mass media, the schools, the churches and the government? Or must we place a large share of blame on inadvertent decadence—on the spiritually debilitating life style into which the Western people have allowed themselves to slip?"

Hard to say, Earl.

The funniest part of this book is that Turner keeps getting indignant when "The Enemy," which intends to turn us all into "a swarming horde of indifferent mulatto zombies," calls the Order "racist." When the Order is decried by the media in this book as "racist and anti-Semitic," Turner considers it unfair!

Sex, of course, rears its ugly head. "Hesitantly, she stepped towards me. Nature took her course." All this is good for women. "Our women are actually cherished and protected to a much larger degree than women in the general society are."

I hold Timothy McVeigh's English teachers responsible for this whole situation. Didn't anyone ever teach the poor boy the difference between a good book and a bad one?

Fort Worth Star-Telegram
August 20, 1995

Look to the Children of the Poor in This Season of Budget-Slashing

A good Christmas column, in my opinion, should be about love, peace, and joy. This one is not. But way back, before shopping malls and eggnog and office parties, back at the very beginning of it all, there was a child, born to very poor people. That's what this Christmas column is about.

"If there is anything more revolting than seeing the rich and shameless celebrating themselves for having the 'courage' to kick the poor and needy in the teeth, it's the unrich and shameless journalist cadres that follow in their wake, celebrating the 'style' with which they do it."—Eric Alterman, *The Nation.* A thought to keep in mind while reading *Time* magazine's Man of the Year profile of House Speaker Newt Gingrich.

When Gingrich has an accusatory fit, it is always instructive. "Anyone who says we are hurting children is lying. Lying! L-Y-I-N-G," Gingrich said recently. Students of Mr. Gingrich will recognize the ploy at once: Don't address the issue—attack the critics.

Among the "liars" is Senator Patrick Moynihan, who has been trying to reform the welfare system since Gingrich was a pup. Moynihan says flatly that those who will pay for "welfare reform" a la Republican are children. For sixty years the Social Security Act has included a section that provides aid for dependent children. Aid to Families with Dependent Children is all that holds millions of families together and off the streets.

How the American right managed to convince itself that the programs to alleviate poverty are responsible for the consequences of poverty will someday be studied as a notorious mass illusion. In the meantime, real children—kids who get earaches and like Big Bird and are crabby when they aren't fed and whose eyes widen in wonder when they meet Santa Claus—will pay the price for this pernicious folly.

An administration study—which the White House tried to suppress—says that 1.2 million *more* children will be pushed into poverty by the Republican proposals. Katha Pollitt writes that "poverty . . . produces in vast quantities addiction, mental illness, domestic violence, social isolation and household chaos." In the name of sanity, does anyone expect to change that by cutting off AFDC after five years? By mandating that states reduce their welfare rolls by 50 percent? Where are the jobs? Who will take care of the children?

Every country in Europe provides basic medical care for all citizens. Medicaid, the health-insurance program for poor people in this country, is being cut. AFDC grants are being capped, which means first come, first served, and anyone who shows up late is out of luck.

One reads the brief, cold, wire-service descriptions of the new regulations and demands: "Teen parent must live at home and attend school to get cash benefits." And when the teen parent was impregnated in the first place by her abusive stepfather? "States prohibited from using federal funds for welfare families that have more children." How many of you were "planned" children?

My favorite is: "Saves $58 billion over seven years." The Center for the Study of Responsive Law reports 153 sources of federal business welfare in the 1995 budget totaling $167.2 billion, or $1,388 per individual taxpayer. All the social-assistance programs, including

AFDC, food stamps, housing assistance, and child nutrition, cost $50 billion per year, or $415 per individual taxpayer. Which do you think is a better investment of your tax dollars: promoting California raisins in Japan so that grape growers can get richer, or giving adequate nutrition to children?

"Saves $58 billion over seven years." Oh, no, it doesn't. Long before AFDC, everyone from Charles Dickens to Jacob Riis agreed on three things about poverty: Slums breed rats, slums breed roaches, and slums breed crime. California, our largest state, is almost at a point where it is spending more on prisons than it does on higher education—a fair working definition of a dead civilization. We already have the highest incarceration rate of any nation on earth—and all of it is wasted money on wasted lives.

All around us carolers sing, "A child, a child, shivers in the cold. Let us bring him silver and gold, let us bring him silver and gold."

Jesus wept.

Fort Worth Star-Telegram
December 24, 1995

Somebody Ought to Tell What
Welfare Reform Will Do

Today's sermon is for the brethren and sistren in the media. Those who like to gripe about them might take pen in hand to write an editor about this one.

The reporting on the welfare-"deform" bill has been awful—story after story after story on the political implications of same. Will President Clinton sign it? Will he veto it? How much will a veto hurt him?

If he vetoes, Bob Dole gets a dandy election issue. If he doesn't veto, the Republicans claim credit for "ending welfare as we know it." Up one side and down the other of the political calculations involved in this minuet have been covered ad nauseum.

There's just one thing the press corps has left out: what's in the welfare bill.

The New York Times has even thoughtfully located the key segment of the citizenry in this debate; it turns out to be the swing voters. "Those voters—slightly younger, slightly poorer, slightly less educated than the average—are among those who deserted the Democrats in the 1994 midterm elections."

Now here's another gripping bit of news from the polls: "Mr. Clinton . . . gets less credit among voters for trying to change welfare than he does on almost any other issue—even one which he flat-out failed." According to the *Times* poll, "49 percent of respondents thought Mr. Clinton had not made a real effort to change welfare, compared to 44 percent who thought he had."

Exultant Republicans now think they have Clinton in what is known in chess as a fork—damned if he does, damned if he doesn't. House Speaker Newt Gingrich, speaking from his well-known perch of moral authority (Newt for pope), said: "The President has an absolute moral obligation to sign this bill."

Well, now that we're up on the political ramifications of the crucial sign-it/veto-it debate, could somebody just tell us what the thing would actually do?

Sure, happy to oblige. It would shove at least one million more American children into poverty. We're always calling ourselves "the richest country in the world." Actually, we're not, but we're still well up there, and we already have almost one quarter of our children being raised in poverty.

The Republican response to what we all dutifully acknowledge is a dreadful welfare system is to get rid of welfare as we know it by making it worse. The illusion of change, you see, is what they are selling in Washington.

But who pays the price? Not these famous swing voters, with their 49–44 perception that Clinton hasn't made a serious effort to change welfare. One. Million. Children.

And the one million children who are directly moved into poverty by this bill are only the beginning of the horror that it is almost guaranteed to create. The House bill eliminates all assured federal funding in cases of child abuse and neglect. Victims of domestic violence and their children will have no assurance that if they escape the violence they can at least survive on cash assistance until they are able to find a job.

Let me tell you something heretical about welfare as we know it: It works just the way we want it to for the vast majority of welfare recipients.

Seventy percent of those who receive welfare get on it and then get off it in far less time than the five-year cutoff in the welfare-deform bill. Of course, that does leave us stuck with the other 30 percent, who get on it and stay—sometimes for one generation after another in the same family. But if all we want to do is budge that 30 percent off welfare, why harm the other 70 percent who use the temporary assistance as it was originally designed to be used?

Under the bills, the federal guarantee of cash assistance for poor children and families is replaced by flat block grants to the states, with a pitifully inadequate provision for extra assistance should recession and unemployment hit. In addition, states are then allowed to cut their own spending on income assistance by 20 percent in the Senate bill, 25 percent in the House bill. Would they do that? Do poor children vote? Could you raise a child on fifteen dollars a week for food, clothing, and shelter?

There is some kind of magical thinking that seizes politicians in election years. "I know how to fix welfare—we'll just require them all to get jobs!" What jobs? The reason that most people are on welfare in the first place is that they can't find jobs—or child care. Or the jobs don't carry health insurance, so when a kid gets sick, his mom has to go back on welfare to get medical treatment for him.

The way this society works is really simple: The shit flows downhill, and the people at the bottom are drowning in it. Every little change that makes it harder for them to climb up means that millions more of them drown. And most of them are children.

Hey, media people—that's the story, stupid.

Fort Worth Star-Telegram
July 28, 1996

We're Pointing the Gun
at Ourselves

In one of those hopeful signs that makes you perk up and think the human race might make it after all, the world's diplomats are meeting in Geneva to see if they can figure out how to ban or at least slow the spread of land mines. Not making much progress, but at least they're meeting.

You've probably heard the arguments—war in poor countries leaves hundreds of thousands of these damn things scattered all over, so that children step on them and kill or cripple themselves for generations after the shooting has stopped. Getting rid of land mines would be an unmitigated good.

Unfortunately, the United States is not in a position to take a high moral tone here, since we're the number-one arms merchant in the world. The old phrase "merchants of death" fits us nicely, thank you. But what's even worse than that is that we taxpayers are subsidizing this dismal trade to the tune of $7.6 billion a year. While Congress is busy cutting welfare to poor American children, we're beefing up welfare for our arms merchants. As they say in the Texas Lege, it's time to rethink our pry-roarities here.

According to a new study funded by the World Policy Institute, which is the offspring of several reputable foundations, total federal subsidies for arms exports jumped from $7 billion in 1994 to $7.6 billion last year. Clinton and the Congress created two new subsidy programs—a $15 billion taxpayer-backed, arms-export loan guarantee fund and a $200 million tax break for foreign arms clients. The United States spends more than $450 million and employs nearly 6,500 full-time people to promote and service foreign arms sales by U.S. companies. The Pentagon has an arms-sales staff of 6,395, an increase of 7.5 percent since 1992.

Since you've never heard anyone running for office say, "Vote for me and I'll use your tax dollars to subsidize weapons manufacturers," you may wonder how this charming arrangement came about. And you will not be amazed to learn that major weapons-exporting firms contributed $14.8 million to congressional candidates from 1990 to 1994. Lockheed and Martin Marietta alone (now merged into Lockheed Martin, the merger generously subsidized by you and me) gave more than $1.1 million to candidates in 1994. The company also contributed $10,000 to help launch Speaker Newt Gingrich's televised lecture series, the one in which he helpfully explained that boys like to hunt giraffes while girls get infections in ditches (you know I'm not making this up: my imagination isn't that good). Major arms-exporting firms have given over $500,000 in soft money to the Republican and Democratic parties for this year's presidential elections, according to Fenton Communications.

The grand result of legal bribery is what is known in political circles as an OPO—Obvious Pay-Off. The taxpayers are now underwriting *one half* of the total value of U.S. arms exports. I don't know about you, but I'd rather underwrite food exports or environmental-technology exports, or, come to think of it, anything else. As it happens, we are last among the industrialized nations in promoting the export of environmental technology, and while we're number one in arms exports, we're also last in terms of GNP in economic aid to developing countries.

The sheer stupidity of this piece of lunacy is nicely illustrated by the last five times we have sent our troops into conflict situations— Panama, Iraq, Somalia, Haiti, and Bosnia. In every case, the forces on the other side had access to U.S. weaponry, training, or military technology. Does the word *self-defeating* ring any bells?

The World Policy Institute study clearly demonstrates that many of the weapons-proliferations threats cited by the CIA and our military intelligence agencies as rationales for increasing U.S. military spending have been exacerbated by our own weapons sales. In other words, we have to spend more to defend against dangerous situations we ourselves have helped create. Does the word *dumb* come to mind?

Lockheed Martin has even gone so far as to cite the easy availability of U.S. fighter planes on the world market as a reason to build the Air Force's next generation of combat aircraft, the F-22. Think about that. At a cost of $160 million a jet, the F-22 will be the most expensive fighter plane ever built. The taxpayers are getting fleeced coming and going on this deal, while Congress cuts food stamps for poor working families.

What can we do about it? (1) Write; (2) Vote; (3) We have got to change the way campaigns are financed, or this madness will continue until our ever more likely extinction. No joke, the ways weapons dealers buy influence in our government is just one example of the way the whole system is screwed up by this insane campaign-financing problem. The people *we* elect and *we* pay to represent *our* interests are, in fact, bought and paid for by corporate special interests who then siphon off our tax money to make higher profits. And in the case of the merchants of death, we get the additional joy of watching our own soldiers get killed by the weapons we subsidize.

Fort Worth Star-Telegram
August 1, 1996

Will Aerospace Companies
Make Off with Santa's Sack?

Why, Santy Claus, you sly old thing, you *shouldn't* have! No, really, Boeing and McDonnell Douglas don't *need* that nice Christmas present you're about to lay on them. What's that you say? You haven't done anything for the Boeing Company lately? Wrong, chump—your tax dollars are about to pay the costs of Boeing's merger with McDonnell. Your very own Christmas gift to the world's largest aerospace company. So sweet of you—most people only think of the Salvation Army at this time of year.

And here's another reason to be proud of your Christmas giving: Boeing promises that "the number of displaced workers will be minimal." I like the sound of *minimal;* I'd just like to know how many thousands of people we're talking about.

When Lockheed married Martin Marietta, $92 million in bonuses—or "triggered compensation," as they say in Corporateland—was handed out to executives and board members. The U.S. government (that's us, sucker) picked up $31 million of that. A mighty minimal thirty thousand workers lost their jobs in that deal, according to *Take the Rich Off Welfare* by Mark Zepezauer and Arthur Naiman.

To date, the Pentagon has spent at least $300 million subsidizing corporate mergers of defense contractors and plans to spend $3 billion more during the next three years, according to a column by Lawrence Korb in *The Christian Science Monitor.* That's not counting Boeing's expected application for "restructuring costs." In theory, these subsidies "promote the rational downsizing of the defense industry." This prize idiocy, payoffs for layoffs, was rejected by the House last session, but the Senate refused to go along.

Now, while we're meditating on Christmas gifts, let us consider who got coal and switches this year. According to the Center on Budget and Policy Priorities, 93 percent of all the entitlement reductions passed by Congress in 1995 and 1996 were in cuts for programs for poor people. This is an appropriately Dickensian plot for the season, don't you think? Ninety-three percent of everything that's been done to balance the budget in this way is being taken out of the pittance of low-income families and individuals.

Of course, not all the news is bad. Michael Ovitz, for example, will receive around $90 million in compensation for leaving the Disney Company after eighteen months of what is widely regarded as an unsatisfactory performance. What does this have to do with cutting programs for poor people? Just part of the zeitgeist, friends, the tenor of our times. Remember when it was not considered incredibly quaint and dated to be concerned about economic and social justice?

Columbia University's study of children and poverty provoked some seasonal clucking last week. Let's try a new approach. Since the reality of one in four American children growing up in poverty does not seem to bother our GOP-controlled Congress, or even our New Democrat president, let's stop trying to wring tears from those stones. Let's hit 'em in the bottom line.

A child born in poverty is more likely to be a low-birth-weight baby, meaning health problems from then on. Lots of increased health-care costs there, fellow citizens. Then, if they don't get adequate nutrition, their brains don't develop properly, so they don't do well in school and are far more likely to drop out.

Stop thinking poor, hungry children with big, sad eyes, like those kids in Keane paintings. Think of millions of feral teenagers loose on the streets, getting into gangs, killing innocent bystanders, dealing drugs, robbing—and then think of the cost of incarcerating them for years at a time.

I give up on trying to get Republicans to feel sympathy for poor children; it just can't be done. We'll have to go with the bottom-line argument and follow up by scaring them to death. Remember, feral teenagers! Wild in the streets! Another 1.1 million children thrown into poverty by welfare reform. If we don't pay one way, we'll pay another.

Fort Worth Star-Telegram
December 17, 1996

Disconnecting Workers from
Their Companies

Fellow Texans, I have been to Seattle in the state of Washington and seen Wonders there. Seattle is the home of ecological correctness, good living, and a lot of coffee junkies.

O.K., so lots of places have environmentalists, the good life, and coffee, but try this: There is a Massage Bar in the Seattle airport. Where people sit down at a bar and get their necks and shoulders massaged.

And I saw a restaurant that specializes in latte and barbecue. Barbecue and latte. I came home immediately.

Also of interest in Seattle is the machinists strike at the Boeing Company, the big airplane-maker. Thirty-two thousand members of the International Association of Machinists and Aerospace Workers have been on strike for over two months.

And with Christmas coming up, the strikers have just voted overwhelmingly to reject a new offer from the company that had the approval of union leaders. The local paper said Boeing's management was just whomperjawed. (*The Seattle Times* didn't actually say "whomperjawed," of course, but only because the editors don't know the word.)

Management was so confident its offer would be accepted, it had already sent out letters welcoming everyone back to work. But 61 percent of the striking machinists said no to a three-year contract offer their own leaders said they should take.

Here's the history on the deal, and I think you'll find it has some lessons for us all.

Boeing went through this same downsizing fad all the big corporations are hot on, but with some better reasons than most. The company was being squeezed during a bidness slump, so it laid off workers, cut benefits, the whole drill.

The union went along with all this because management promised that when times got better, it would share with the workers. Times got better, but nothing else happened, except, of course, the big executives made out like bandits.

In the past few years, Boeing has laid off tens of thousands of workers. Productivity is up by 30 percent, and the after-tax profit since 1990 is $6.6 billion.

This is an example of what the financial writers genteelly refer to as the "disconnect" between profits and wages. Profits keep going up—and up and up and up—and productivity is at an all-time high, but wages just sit there, quietly shrinking.

This is going on all over the country and is at the root of the political unrest that our esteemed leaders address by tut-tutting about the family values of people on welfare. There is more than one form of "disconnect" going on here.

So, the machinists went out on strike. The company made an offer, the strikers turned it down. Then the company got real and offered a thirty-cent-an-hour cost-of-living allowance, worth $450 in the first nine months, a five-buck increase in monthly pension benefits, and a 3 percent general-wage increase in the third year of the contract, along with a one-time lump-sum payment.

Machinists make an average of $20.37 an hour (eat your hearts out, Texans; they got unions up there), so they're looking at $22.16 an hour after three years, plus $3,100 in the lump-sum payment. And the machinists said no. Gutsy call.

Look, 3 percent after three years is going to be eaten by inflation, and these people have already been nibbled to death for years. According to local labor scholars, the vote was the direct result of one factor—the workers don't trust the company, and they don't trust their own union. Gee, what a surprise.

In a related matter, the always valuable *Wall Street Journal* reported recently that big corporations are atwitter because their trade secrets are suddenly leaking as though the companies were sieves. It seems the problem is that employees are leaking secrets because "they no longer feel a sense of loyalty to the company." Gosh, isn't that amazing?

Twenty years of being laid off, cut back, downsized, right-sized, and left with a paycheck that won't buy what it did in 1975, and suddenly there's a loyalty problem. Boeing keeps shipping jobs overseas, and suddenly there's a trust problem. Imagine that.

Real wages dropped 2.3 percent between March 1994 and March 1995, the biggest drop in eight years, according to the Labor Department. And all we read about is that the economy is doing great and the stock market is over 5,000. Whoopee.

I like the attitude of these Seattle machinists. According to their paper, they've sort of amazed themselves and are feeling pretty proud, even though two months of strike will put you close to the edge. Been there.

So a good chunk of my Christmas charity money this year is going to their strike fund, because I think they're making a stand for more than just themselves.

Fort Worth Star-Telegram
December 5, 1995

How Do Corporations Fit into America's Public Life?

ROCHESTER, N.Y. — Aunt Susan B. Anthony is buried in the town cemetery here, not far from her friend Frederick Douglass. What a hotbed of reformers this place was 150 years ago. Today it's a corporate city. Rochester used to be known as Kodak's company town, but then came Xerox, Bausch & Lomb, Gannett.

Thinking about what those nineteenth-century reformers would be crusading about if they were around today, it seems to me that the most likely answer is the dominant force in their hometown: corporations. Not that Kodak, Xerox, and B&L are bad corporate citizens; to the contrary, they support local arts programs and all manner of community endeavors. Still, Aunt Susan was never one to be misled by window dressing or pretty rhetoric. When she started, both God and Nature were assumed to be aligned in the subjugation of women.

What a curious entity a corporation is—a legal artifact that exists to make a profit. Yet the law views a corporation as a person. The initial constitutional view of corporations as persons was limited to the right to sue and to be sued, which makes perfect economic sense for contract law. But starting in 1948, a series of Supreme Court decisions have given corporations other individual liberties as well. For example, it has been held that corporations have a right to privacy—a right to which women still have only a contested claim. Aunt Susan would have turned incandescent over that one.

The civil rights of corporations are so strong that the entities are now the major political players in this country. Almost two thirds of the money that puts people into federal office today comes from corporations. They effectively elect our government—certainly more effectively than the people do. And as a consequence, the corporations now have more power than the people of this country. That is why the burden of taxation in America has shifted so dramatically from corporations to individual citizens, along with causing a thousand other ills.

The long struggle of the nineteenth-century reformers finally bore fruit in the early twentieth century, with a spurt of progressive/populist legislation that gave the people back some power over corporations—the eight-hour workday, health and safety regulations, anti-trust laws.

But a quick read of any issue of *The Wall Street Journal* will prove that the corporations have shrugged through the restraints and are running loose again, and on a much larger scale. Check the *WSJ* any day for how many of the business stories involve economic globalization—progress thereon, hitches thereto, results thereof.

Those who question the wisdom of economic globalization led by megacorporations are left looking a little quaint. Economic nationalism has a slightly musty flavor, "Buy American" is an old union slogan, and there certainly is a retrograde element to some economic nationalism—immigrant-bashing, for example.

All the trendy people favor NAFTA and GATT and the alphabet soup of free-trade endeavors. Ralph Nader's almost the only citizen left who will stand up and bash corporations about their collective head with a two-by-four. And we know what *The Wall Street Journal* thinks of Nader.

There used to be two basic remedies that the citizen had against an evil-doing corporation. One was government regulation—the govern-ment had the power to step in and stop their depredations, whether against public health, public safety, or the environment. But now the government is effectively a wholly owned subsidiary of corporate power, in the hands of people to whom *regulation* is a dirty word. The Republicans took over Congress promising to drastically reduce the terrible "burden of regulation" that afflicts our poor corporations.

A citizen's other option was to use his Constitution-given right to sue the slime balls. If a corporation sold you something that killed your child or dumped its toxic waste in your backyard, you could get your day in court. But now the corporations are mounting an all-out assault on this remedy as well. They spend millions to influence pub-lic opinion in favor of "tort reform," a charming euphemism that sim-ply means "citizens lose their rights," particularly our right of access to our own courts.

None of this is to say that corporations are intrinsically evil. They are simply legal entities to create profits, and they are genetically pro-grammed, as it were, to increase profits—and more and more they focus on short-term profits only. This is neither good nor evil—it sim-ply is.

The question is what we the people, who have spent more than two hundred years working slowly toward greater liberty and justice for all, should do with these powerful entities now shaping our lives and our polity. Corporations are not concerned with economic justice or with social justice—it's not their job. It is our job. And we need to start thinking hard about how we integrate these strange legal entities into the scheme.

Fort Worth Star-Telegram
December 15, 1996

Dumped by Disney

I'm apparently up for sale this morning, along with my newspaper, the *Fort Worth Star-Telegram.* Our corporate masters have put us on the bidding block, and here we stand, waiting for prospective buyers to come along and inspect our teeth, as it were.

As a veteran of this experience (this is my fourth time on the block), I prefer it when the corporate masters announce the results abruptly after the deed is done. That way you don't have time to worry about which Simon Legree might come along and snap you up as a bargain at the price. "Could have been worse," we say to one another after the done deal is announced. "We could have gone to Rupert Murdoch." Mr. Murdoch is widely regarded as the worst plantation owner producing our particular crop.

Trouble is, the news business is rapidly becoming one big plantation. I'm looking over the list of potential bidders the same way they're looking over us. Newhouse is on the list. Murray Kempton once observed, "I think Si Newhouse has lost his moral compass since Roy Cohn died"—the single meanest thing I've ever heard said about anyone.

Gannett still means Al Neuharth; I always thought he was a dipstick. A. H. Belo Corporation? I once swore that pigs would fly before I'd work for Belo, which owns *The Dallas Morning News.* Besides, Amon Carter, Sr., former patriarch of the *Star-Telegram,* is gonna come up out of his grave if that happens. When Carter was forced to go to Dallas, which he cordially loathed, he reportedly always carried his own lunch in a brown paper bag so as not to contribute to the economy of Big D.

Amon senior has been on my mind lately. I was out in Big Bend over New Year's: few people remember it now, but Amon senior was the driving force behind getting the Bend made into a park in the first place. He loved West Texas and started a drive to raise the money to pay for the park. Used the *Star-Telegram* to crusade for it, too. The new corporate masters don't do things like that; we're on the block because our division is producing a profit of only $200 million this year. That barely covers Michael Ovitz's golden parachute. Yesterday the Walt Disney Company announced a 33 percent increase in its net income in the first quarter of fiscal '97.

According to the business pages, Disney faces a huge tax bite by selling off its newspapers; some monster capital-gains tab comes due. But apparently they think it's worth it, because they're teaming up with Comcast Corporation to acquire control of E! Entertainment Television. And how can the *Star-Telegram* compete with E! Entertainment TV? We're just a pretty good paper with a couple of Pulitzers to our credit. We've broken some important stories and gone after some local biggies, but let's face it: The *Star-Telegram* doesn't know squat about Brad Pitt's love life. We still think tax increases in Arlington are a story.

I'm teaching a course now to some of the world's brightest graduate students, trying to convince them that journalism is an honorable and important craft. We talk a lot about what citizens need to know in order to participate in running their own country properly.

We discuss ethical traps and libel and fairness, the morality of writing about the private lives of public figures, and the corruption of the political system by money. We talk about how to get people interested in public affairs, how to report on the public's business without squeezing out all the life and suspense and juice and joy and humor of it. We even talk about just societies and equal opportunity. And of course we study the media themselves, the new sources of information, the new technologies. And the concentration of ownership of the media and its effect on what we do.

The dean emeritus of the journalism school at U.C.-Berkeley is Ben Bagdikian, perhaps the foremost scholar of the phenomenon, author of *Media Monopoly*.

I've never had much use for management myself. I've worked for a wide variety of managements, and the result is that I always join a union if there's one available. When management was the art of getting a whole bunch of people together to do something in the best way possible, I had some interest in it. But now that it has become an endless quest for increased quarterly profits, I find it boring and a menace to quality.

I suppose that we of the *Star-Telegram* and our sister papers, with our piddly $200 million profit, could feel some sense of rejection at being dumped by the mighty Disney Company, with its 33 percent increase and acquisition of E! TV. But being dumped by the people who hired Michael Ovitz and then paid $90 million to get rid of him doesn't strike me as a great humiliation.

A year ago, this genius manager Michael Eisner assured all the newspapers in our group that his company was in publishing to stay. In the newspaper trade, which has never been genteel, we call that lying. Personally, I think we're just as well off being dumped out of that frying pan.

Fort Worth Star-Telegram
January 30, 1997

To Observe and Protect

The feisty little magazine the *Texas Observer* is known to almost everyone inside Texas politics and journalism and known to practically no one outside. The *Observer,* now forty-three years old, recently had a near-death experience, and although the prognosis is cheerful, the episode makes a telling point about American journalism today.

The *Observer* has always been a scrappy, progressive, hell-raising, muckraking little publication devoted to coverage of Texas politics and social issues, with a little culture thrown in at the "back of the book." In the fifties, sixties, and even much of the seventies, the *Observer* was unique in bucking against the old conservative Democratic establishment in the days when this was a one-party state. And it was unique in its concern for black folks and brown folks in Texas.

There wasn't an establishment newspaper in the state that would even condescend to write about their concerns, much less champion their efforts to win justice. But as the daily newspapers gradually improved and a few other magazines started up around the state, the *Observer*'s role as the one and only crusader for social justice gradually diminished.

Although the *Observer* hasn't changed much over the years, today it is unique not so much for what it is as for what it is not. It is not owned by a corporation, it is not for-profit, and it is not dependent on advertisers. It remains, as it says on the masthead, "A Journal of Free Voices." That makes it increasingly valuable and increasingly fragile.

Just a few facts about the concentration of ownership of the media in this country: Although the country had long known newspaper barons like Hearst and Scripps, at the end of World War II the great majority of media outlets were still independently owned. By 1982, fifty corporations controlled almost all of the major media outlets in the United States: 1,787 daily newspapers, 11,000 magazines, 9,000 radio stations, 1,000 TV stations, 2,500 book publishers, and 7 major movie studios.

Five years later, that was down to twenty-nine corporations. Today, it is fewer than twenty. And the impetus toward concentration continues; in fact, it is accelerating, and it includes the new media outlets such as cable and on-line ventures.

With corporate ownership comes increased pressure for profits, and with the pressure for profits comes increased pressure from advertisers. The "wall of separation" between advertising and editorial content, which has long distinguished our best journalism, is increasingly being breached.

That fact is the talk of our business; it has been covered in *The Wall Street Journal* and on National Public Radio. Jonathan Alter wrote an excellent essay about it in *Newsweek*. Chrysler Corporation, for example, requires written summaries of all articles in any magazine that will carry its ads. Other companies have laundry lists of taboo subjects. After a recent disagreement with the editors at *Esquire* magazine (the editors lost), Chrysler spelled out its requirements: The company must "be alerted in advance of any and all editorial content that encompasses sexual, political, social issues, or any editorial that might be construed as provocative or offensive."

Chrysler, of course, claims that it is not engaging in censorship—it merely wants to place its advertisements "in the most positive atmo-sphere possible."

I think back to the old days at the *Observer,* when it was the only paper in the state that would carry a story headlined, "Consequences of a Dance," here reprinted in its entirety:

AUG. 21, 1959—An instance of interracial dancing in Elge Brown's cafe on what some local whites call "nigger hill" in Gatesville has spun off serious consequences for the six people involved and is still spinning.

A cedar chopper and his wife, who consented to their 12 and 14-year-old daughters dancing with some Negro men in their middle twenties, have served out their 70 days in the Coryell County jail in Gatesville, but they have lost custody of their daughters. The girls were first sent to Gainesville State School, the reformatory for delinquent girls, but authorities there decided they were not delin-quents and sent them to the state home for neglected children in Corsicana, where they are living now, six months after the episode. One of the Negro men, charged with aggravated assault, paid $100 and costs on a guilty plea. The other has got himself a lawyer to resist the complaint against him on the same count.

The complaint against each of the Negroes charged him with "placing his arms and hands around her and squeezing and holding her, rubbing his face against hers."

I suspect the Chrysler Corporation would not then or now consider that "the most positive atmosphere possible" for its advertisements. But I'm proud that the *Observer* ran such stories back then, and I'm glad that it's still around today to report on recent episodes, such as how the KuKluxKlanner got elected county commissioner in Val Verde, and how big corporations are trying to use Texas as a toxic-waste dump, and how the cow ate the cabbage in the Legislature.

After forty-three years of surviving largely on subscription income, the *Observer* has finally learned what every other political magazine in

America figured out a long time ago: It can't be done. To remain independent of advertisers, political magazines must have either a wealthy backer, like William F. Buckley, Jr., of *The National Review,* or they must build in a permanent fund-raising component, just like a university. The *Observer* is now engaged in building an endowment that will keep it independent.

I have a dog in this fight: I served as coeditor of the *Observer* with Kaye Northcott, now also of the *Fort Worth Star-Telegram,* from 1970 to 1976. I regard that little magazine as my alma mater, the most important teaching institution of my life. I still believe that the purpose of journalism is to comfort the afflicted and to afflict the comfortable. I can think of few causes more important than keeping free voices alive in a world of corporate media.

I think of my years at the *Observer* the way some folks think of their college years: a happy, golden time, full of sunshine and laughter and beer. No one who has ever worked for the *Observer* made much money at it, but we never thought money was particularly important at the *Observer.* We liked to root for the good guys and nail the bad guys. Nailed quite a few of them, too—ask Ben Barnes. LBJ used to cuss "those *Observer* boys" somethin' awful—even when the boys were girls.

Think of almost any Texas writer you've heard of in the last fifty years, and you'll find that almost every one of them either worked for or wrote for the *Observer:* Willie Morris, J. Frank Dobie, Billy Lee Brammer, Larry Goodwyn, Larry L. King, Larry McMurtry, Jim Hightower, et cetera.

We never had any money, so we used to travel the state on a sort of underground railroad. Clif Olafson, our beloved business manager, would provide us with a list of subscribers in whatever direction we were headed. Come sundown, we'd stop and call the nearest subscriber. The invariable response was: "From the *Observer*? Gosh, can you come over for a beer, can you stay for dinner, can you stay the night?" And they'd call the other two liberals in town, and the four of us would have a whale of a party.

We were so poor at the *Observer* that Clif used to sleep under the Addressograph. I stole pencils from the governor's office. (They said STATE OF TEXAS and had the seal on 'em—very nice pencils.) We got some of our best stories because that's where our cars happened to break down.

In addition to crusading for Truth, Justice, and the American Way, *Observer* editors tend to have an unseemly amount of fun. Let's face it: The Great State has a large loony streak, and it has always been the delight of the *Observer* to chronicle the more ludicrous aspects of life in the Lone Star.

The time two Republicanesses duked it out at a meeting of the state Republican Executive Committee remains my all-time favorite bout—even better than the last all-House duke-out in the Lege, when our elected representatives threw chairs and chili dogs at one another while a barbershop quartet sang "I Have A Dream, Dear": That was the duke-out that caused them to ban food on the floor of the House.

Larry Goodwyn, a former editor and the great historian of the populist movement, once called the *Observer* the finest graduate school of journalism in America. That's because the *Observer*'s standards were set by its founding editor, Ronnie Dugger. Dugger is both committed to social justice and the most incurably fair reporter I ever knew. I'm not claiming that all the succeeding editors have lived up to Dugger's standards, but he sure set 'em high.

The *Observer* changes a bit as it goes from editor to editor. Some have been a little doctrinaire, some (like *moi*) relished the comedy more, while others emphasized the arts. Hightower's *Observer* was like a loaf of that whole-grain bread; you knew it was good for you. But the meat and potatoes of the magazine has always been Texas politics. The incumbent editor, Lou DuBose, is bilingual and has more good stuff on Mexico and South Texas than you can get anywhere else.

Our state will become majority-minority in just a few short years, and Chicanos will be the dominant group. You think you're reading anything now that's getting you ready for what that will be like? Try the *Texas Observer.*

What you won't find in the *Observer* is stories tailored for yuppies, the famous "upscale reader" so loved by advertisers. The *Observer* doesn't do Ten Best Barbecue Joints or Ten Best Ice Cream Parlors. The *Observer* won't teach you how to be a consumer. It's not in business to make more money for its advertisers.

This is what the *Observer* claims as its goal: "We will serve no group or party but will hew hard to the truth as we find it and the right as we see it. We are dedicated to the whole truth, to human values above all interests, to the rights of humankind as the foundation of democracy, we will take orders from none but our own conscience, and never will we overlook or misrepresent the truth to serve the interests of the powerful or cater to the ignoble in the human spirit."

And that's why, in the words of those bumper stickers we see around the state, my kids (students) and my money are going to the *Texas Observer.* I hope yours will, too. The address is www.texasobserver.org.

Fort Worth Star-Telegram
July 20, 1997

Dear Fundamentalists: Tolerance Is Not a Dirty Word

I'm getting so tired of this fundamentalist censorship racket. Donald Wildmon and his merry band of bluenoses at the American Family Association (puh-leeze) are at it again, this time spreading a twelve-minute videotape of selected moments from the PBS hit series *Tales of the City.* They carefully excerpted all the "dirty bits" and are sending them around for everyone's salacious enjoyment and to prevent PBS from making a sequel to the popular series.

It's as though someone were to tell you, "Molly Ivins wrote a column today using the words *cock, prick, pussy, ass, breast, balls, tit,* and *dong.*" Without saying how they were used, as in:

"That darn cock started crowing a five o'clock this morning: I like to got out my BB gun."

"Take this needle and prick all those balloons so we can finish cleaning up and get out of here—I swear this is the last time I ever volunteer for cleanup committee after a dance."

"The poor little pussycat was chased up a tree by that rotten rottweiler, and now I can't get her to come down: I think she's traumatized."

"According to the Bible, Mary rode on an ass into Bethlehem."

"I know you can't see it from here in the trough, but all you have to do is breast the next wave and you'll see the shore."

"It was all those bases on balls that cost us the game."

"I told him I operate on a tit-for-tat basis and he could expect a payback from me."

"Why don't you replace that tinny old ding-dong bell with an electric buzzer?"

In art, context is everything. And this column ain't even close to art.

In a recent essay on Molière, the critic David Richards wrote, "Today, most mainstream comedy falls into the realm of toothless situation comedy. It springs from misunderstandings, not irreconcilable differences; from irritating habits, not character flaws; from pique, not outrage. Smuttiness is thought daring when it is merely a cowardly form of scatology. Television has done as much as anything to castrate the form. The times officially subscribe to good taste, political correctness and fair play—all of which inhibit comedy's defiant spirit. Sickness is judged no laughing matter and religion is off-limits, except perhaps for those grinning evangelists who mock themselves."

It's a shame Molière and the Reverend Donald Wildmon missed each other by three centuries, because Molière could have used him. As Richards also wrote, "As writer and actor, he portrayed the obstinate will better than anybody before or since. That's one reason he continues to seem astonishingly modern. So many of history's catastrophes, and just as many personal misfortunes, have been brought about by unbending creatures kicking compromise and reason aside and barreling full force into a brick wall. Molière gives us the disaster as high comedy, all-knowing patriarchs as hilariously petty dictators, inflexibility as the funniest of all human substances."

Why Wildmon and his organization don't pick on all the tawdry, third-rate smut on television is beyond me: why do they have to go attack one of the few successful, original pieces of art on American television? Maybe we should start using them as a reverse rating index—anything they criticize must be worth watching.

Just last week I learned the MMPI (Minnesota Multiphasic Personality Inventory), the diagnostic tool used by psychologists, can spot two personality traits without fail. The MMPI is so respected that it is now used by many police forces around the country to screen out candidates who shouldn't be allowed loose with a gun. The two behavior patterns the MMPI reveals are rule-breaking in a way that can and often does lead to criminal behavior and . . . fundamentalism. Maybe the shrinks should consider declaring it a personality disorder.

One of the problems we have as a society in dealing with fundamentalists is that the larger society values tolerance but fundamentalists don't. We're prepared to tolerate them and their behavior, and they're not prepared to return the favor. (A wise friend of mine once observed that he didn't care for the word *tolerance* because it smacks of condescension. "I tolerate you" means "I deign to recognize your right to exist." He could be right: Tolerance is not respect.)

I persist in thinking that fundamentalists are misunderstood, frightened (with some cause), and generally get damned little of the empathy and compassion on which we liberals so pride ourselves. I also think they shouldn't be allowed to touch the Constitution or even PBS. Liberals have this revolting tendency toward reasonable compromise: "I mean, really, what harm is some nondenominational prayer in the schools going to do anyone? Or a moment of silence, for heaven's sake?" Trouble is, we're compromising with people who don't understand compromise. Tolerance, inadequate though it may be, is still an absolute requirement in a democracy.

Fort Worth Star-Telegram
April 18, 1994

Nobody Gets Cut Any Slack
for Their Political Passion

"So, Bill," says I to my old pal Murchison of the *Morning News* in the middle of the Texas Republican Convention, "what do you think of the Christian right?" This was just after the Christian right had defeated a resolution encouraging civility.

"Oh, I think they bring passion to politics and that's not a bad thing," says Murchison, one of the most personally decent right-wing nuts in America. "The party could use a little passion."

Likewise, Michael Kinsley, the neoliberal guru, wrote last week that the Clinton administration should take a dive on getting abortion covered by the new health-care plan because its opponents are so "passionate." I've always been in favor of zip and idealism in politics, as opposed to the deadly little apparatchiks who think politics is about winning, period. But we need to think about what George Bush would call "the passion thing."

There were a lot of passionate people at the convention in Fort Worth last weekend who may yet give fanaticism a bad name. Remember when Barry Goldwater said, "Extremism in the defense of liberty is no vice . . ."? These people think Barry Goldwater is a liberal wimp.

Katha Pollitt of *The Nation* said in response to Kinsley's essay, "Should we too murder our opponents and set fire to their buildings? Phone daily bomb threats to those phony clinics and 'problem pregnancy centers,' scream obscenities at the staff, picket their homes and stalk their children? Flaunt the corpses of abandoned newborns, like the pro-life minister who tried to give Candidate Clinton a dead fetus? . . . If I have to choose between forcing pro-lifers to have qualms and forcing 15-year-olds to have babies, I know which side I'm on."

As Pollitt points out, backing down on abortion rights because those opposed to them are so "passionate" is a way of rewarding terrorism. And the terrorism of the anti-choice movement is just as real as the terrorism of those who bombed the World Trade Center.

Although the literature of the Christian right is full of their goal of "Christianizing government," their candidates have learned to avoid that phrase when talking to the media. "Well," said one, "the people who founded this country were Christians." No, they weren't. Many of the Founding Fathers were Deists, now called Unitarians, who believed in God but not in the divinity of Jesus. I got out the Jefferson Bible the other day, the one Jefferson put together himself from two Greek translations of the Bible, two English translations, one French, and two Latin. In the introduction, I found this quote: "It is in our lives and not our words that our religion must be read."

Jefferson believed Jesus' "system of morality was the most benevolent and sublime . . . ever taught, and consequently more perfect than those of any of the ancient philosophers." But in regard to the fundamentalists of his day, he wrote, "They believe that any portion of power confided to me will be exerted in opposition to their schemes. And they believe rightly; for I have sworn upon the altar of God, eternal hostility against any form of tyranny over the mind of man."

Religious zealots are nothing new in our political life, but cutting them slack because of the perfervidness of their beliefs is perfect folly.

It is precisely their zealotry, their unwillingness to compromise, and their intolerance that makes them unfit for political office. The Republican party has nominated six candidates for the state Board of Education, all from the religious right; four of them are home-schoolers and two send their children to private schools. Does it make any sense at all to put these people in charge of the curriculum in the public schools? I'm sorry, but just because the Bible says something does not make it true: the world is not six thousand years old—recorded history runs longer than that. The Bible instructs us to "take up snakes," yet I could find no snake-handlers among the committed Christians in Fort Worth last weekend. But they are prepared to demand that belief in biblical inerrancy be required of all schoolteachers.

Politically, the Republican party is now facing exactly the same fight the Baptist General Convention has been going through for several years, including many of the same players. You will recall that the conservatives ousted the moderates in the General Convention over a series of years, gradually taking increasingly close control of all Baptist institutions. The religious right now has control of the levers of the Republican-party machinery, but it does not have control of the party's top candidates—Phil Gramm, George Bush, and Kay Bailey Hutchison are not religious fanatics, so the public perception of the party as a tool of the religious right will be delayed.

I would bet that two years from now, when people go to party precinct meetings in support of their various presidential candidates, the religious right will be set back in the number of delegates it controls. But I would also bet that the religious right is in this fight for the long haul, and Republicans who think they can "Take It Back," as they call their party movement, had best be prepared to fight for a long time and with great tenacity. And, I might add, passion.

Fort Worth Star-Telegram
June 16, 1994

Peace on Earth?
Not as Long as There's a
Creche Controversy

PITTSBURGH — First annual sighting of the creche controversy! Hooray, hoorah—the festive, seasonal creche controversy is back, with the first specimen of the year showing up in beautiful downtown Pittsburgh. How we all enjoy the annual fistfight over how to salute Peace on Earth and Goodwill Toward Men.

Every year, in an excess of seasonal exuberance, some citizen—in this case the Diocesan Holy Name Society—decides to display a Nativity scene in a prominent public place. A lovely idea, enjoyed by all. Alas, some other citizens always decide that the perfect place for said Nativity scene is the center of some government building, in this case the Allegheny County Courthouse. Judging from the sound of the Allegheny County commissioners, the Nativity scene may be the only way they'll ever get three wise men in that building.

It seems that the county commissioners have already been through this mill once and didn't learn a damn thing. In 1989 the courthouse Nativity scene was declared unconstitutional after the U.S. Supreme Court decided that the county government was, in effect, promoting the Christian religion. But Commissioners Dunn and Cranmer (locally known as "Dumb and Dumber") have decided to once more test the strength of the court's determination to keep government out of religion. The Supremes have declared in recent cases that religious symbols may be displayed along with secular Christmas symbols, so we are now down to debating degrees of decoration.

For example, if jolly Old Saint Nick is coming down the chimney to greet Baby Jesus, and Rudolph the Red-Nosed Reindeer is dancing on the roof with some of the attendant sheep, will the display pass? If we throw in a menorah and some stuff from Kwanzaa, will it be O.K.? Or are we addling our poor children's minds and creating theological and cultural hash?

The Supremes have further muddied the water by saying that government property can be used to display religious symbols if the public property in question is a traditional site for public expressions of sentiment. (The case in question involved a cross put up in a Columbus, Ohio, park by the Ku Klux Klan. Fortunately, the Kluckers didn't burn it, they too having succumbed to seasonal goodwill. We live in a great nation.)

I once found a splendid display of secular seasonal celebration in the main post office in Adelaide, Australia. It was a six-foot statue of a kangaroo wearing a Santa hat, with dark glasses on (Christmas comes in summer there) and a present in her pouch. Christmas trees are acceptable in all locales, although the churches may want to reconsider the tree tradition, which originally came from pagan Germans.

Personally, I don't worry about the cultural confusion of children created by such phenomena as Santy at the manger, an arrangement I first saw in a Dallas lawn display. It's my impression that most children go through a period of thinking Gladly the Cross-Eyed Bear is the Son of God, but they generally get it straightened out eventually—resilient creatures.

The regular villain in the creche controversy is the American Civil Liberties Union, playing its assigned role as the Grinch in the case with weary resignation. Few things will make you less popular than suing someone at Christmastime for unseemly religious display. Every year I beg them, "Couldn't you wait till after New Year's?" But no, every year they insist on reminding us of all this tiresome separation-of-church-and-state stuff. You know who thought that stuff up, don't you? Those pesky Founding Fathers.

In fact, one of them, James Madison, actually wrote down why they did it. "The purpose of separation of church and state is to keep forever from these shores the ceaseless strife that has soaked the soil of Europe with blood for centuries."

Oh. That. Like, perhaps, the soil of Bosnia, still wet with blood, some of it apparently from Muslim virgins who were raped as a matter of policy by their Christian neighbors? That kind of ceaseless strife?

That our own ceaseless strife comes down to these silly creche cases every Christmas is a tribute to the genius of the founders. I suggest that we continue to observe their precious separation for precisely the reason that Mr. Madison cited. It's a principle of some importance. It's even worth having the ACLU be a pain in the butt about it every Christmas.

We might even avoid the annual lawsuits over it if we all acted like grown-ups and saved our religious displays for private property.

Ho-ho-ho.

Fort Worth Star-Telegram
November 14, 1996

No Way O.J. Ends Up Having to Take That Final Walk

Airports are not great places in which to observe human spontaneity; except for the folks who turn out to meet their loved ones or the occasional harried traveler who blows up at a ticket clerk, they're mostly full of preoccupied zombies. So when I was leaving New York via JFK a few months back, I was startled to hear a ruckus developing behind me.

Down the long linoleum corridor lit by fluorescent lights sprinted a white businessman going flat-out. The guy looked like an ad in *Forbes,* gray hair, silver at the temples, impeccably dressed and flying full tilt, briefcase under his arm, shouting: "Look out, I'm doing an O.J.! Look out, I'm doing an O.J.!" Onlookers started clapping and yelling, "Go, go, go! Go, Juice!" Those of us at the end of the corridor got to see him sprint into the on-ramp, legs still pumping high, with maybe three seconds to spare before the door slammed shut and we gave him a round of applause.

We have such a hard time accepting tragedy in this country. We're on a steady diet of movies and TV shows with happy endings, with only an occasional night of Shakespeare, O'Neill, or some gloomy

Scandinavian to remind us that life is not a Hallmark card. The denial of death is such an intrinsic part of our culture that sometimes the only people who seem like grown-ups are those in, as they say, "the AIDS community."

So the first thing people wanted was someone to blame. Who let him get away? Why didn't the cops have him under surveillance? Why did the district attorney take so long to file against him? Yadda, yadda, yadda. All this being played out against one of the most surreal nights in our national life ("How are the Rockets doing? Did they catch him yet? Did he kill himself yet?").

I happened to be at a convention of the National Society of Newspaper Columnists (yes, we actually have one), where, naturally, no one could stop commenting as the thing unfolded. In the other room, a few of the brothers watched the Rockets-Knicks game on a fancy TV set that had the car chase playing simultaneously in a corner of the screen—truly surreal.

Remember the time Patty Hearst was kidnapped by the Symbionese Liberation Army, and we all watched the shootout on television and their house burned in front of our eyes? Remember watching the Branch Davidian compound blaze away, live and in color? Remember when Jack Ruby shot Lee Harvey Oswald, not so much in the stomach as on television? Boy, that Reality Theater, it really gets the ratings, doesn't it?

And now the story will have a surprise ending after all. All through the day O. J. Simpson was missing, people kept saying: "He's a dead man. Either the cops get him or he does it himself." The cops themselves were most afraid of "suicide by cop," where he comes out with a gun and they have to shoot him. But whatever happens to Simpson in the criminal-justice system, he is not going to be a dead man; this is one double-murder suspect who will not end up in "The Chamber." And here, friends, for all of you who have been searching so earnestly for some moral to this tragedy, as though tragedy had a moral, here's one you can seize with both hands and your teeth.

All you death-penalty advocates out there, listen to yourselves talk about Simpson. Came from the projects, grew up without a father, got involved with a teenage gang, never would have had a chance if he hadn't been so gifted. All the stress that success puts on a guy like that, justice system should have done something about the domestic violence early on, pain of a broken marriage. "She probably drove him crazy," said one of the sternest death-penalty advocates I know.

No way does O. J. Simpson, who may yet even be acquitted, get the death penalty. If you were on the jury, you wouldn't consider it even with DNA evidence, would you? He's rich, he's got a great lawyer, he's famous, he's even a nice guy most of the time.

All that is fine with me. All I want you to admit is that, except for psychopaths and sociopaths who belong in mental hospitals, everyone on death row is just like O. J. Simpson except not rich or famous. They always come from backgrounds where "they never had a chance"—and no one else has ever been able to run like O.J.—and then something happened, and they screwed up their lives and killed someone . . . and killing them doesn't change a thing.*

Fort Worth Star-Telegram
June 21, 1994

* This was the last time I ever wrote about the O. J. Simpson case.

And We Still Must Do
the Best That We Can

Suppose you went on a vacation where no one could reach you—say, rafting the Colorado River. Day after day of vivid blue skies, puffy clouds, red sandstone cliffs in fantastic formations. No Rwanda, no Haiti, no O.J., no lobbyists swarming over health-care reform like maggots. Just soaring golden eagles, great blue herons, bighorn sheep, canyon wrens, and a coyote. Just long stretches of river mellow, occasionally punctuated by the excitement of white water—white water with no political connotation.

Would the world be any worse off for your not knowing that cholera has broken out among the Rwandan refugees in Zaire? The trouble with global communications is that it is no longer possible to sit on one tiny patch of the earth and think, "God's in His heaven, all's right with the world." We always know better.

As a journalist, I'm committed to the proposition that it is always better to know than to be ignorant. Reluctantly, grudgingly, I even acknowledge that television—root of much evil, opiate of the masses, eroder of the national IQ—allows us to know some things with the impact of reality, in a way no other medium can. If it were not for television, would "massive aid" be on its way to Rwanda this morning? No.

I hear them on the radio call-in shows: "What do we care what happens in Rwanda?" But then television shows us what is happening, and we rise from our Barca-Loungers to call the representative, write the check to Oxfam, find the address for Doctors Without Borders. Even my beloved former colleague Ray Bonner, writing from Zaire in *The New York Times* about the tiny girl in the pink dress sitting next to the body of her mother, moves one to tears, not action.

All the weekend chat shows will be denouncing "television-driven foreign policy" again, as though healing the sick and feeding the starving were some fluffy liberal notion to be deplored by the Kissingerian realists, as though "Let those people die" were realpolitik. You still reap what you sow in this world; there is still a moral imperative to help where you can—and to hate the hate, hate the bigotry, hate the racism, hate the fear and the ignorance that leave two more tiny girls sitting next to the tiny one in the pink dress by her dead mother the next day.

The very technology, the global communication that disturbs us in our recliners, also makes it possible for us to send "massive aid" that arrives in a day, two days, a week. John Donne taught us that no man is an island, and Marshall McLuhan taught us that no nation is an island.

I've always suspected that this was apocryphal, but George Washington once supposedly remarked: "We haven't heard from Ben Franklin in Paris yet this year. We ought to send him a letter." Sure, and it must have been an easier world then, with more time to think about what Franklin had to report and what to do about it. "Let's wait and see what develops" is, I have always thought, one of the great foreign-policy options. But we don't live in Washington's and Franklin's world, and we still have to do the best we can.

"If we have an obligation in Rwanda, then surely we have a greater obligation in Haiti; and if in Haiti, then why not Bosnia?" For those of us who are of the Vietnam generation, the terrible blunder made with good intentions (or even out of Kissingerian realpolitik) holds a particular horror. You don't even have to remember 'Nam—try the Marine barracks in Beirut in '84 or Somalia in '93. But we still have to do the best we can.

A British journalist who covered the most recent Ethiopian famine told me what it was like in the camps there. "You get up every day and you do as much as you can," said Rod Tyler of the *Daily Mail.* "You carry bags of grain or ladle water or dig latrines, or whatever the relief workers ask you to do. And in the midst of all those starving people, you have to eat three meals a day, and you have to sleep at least six or seven hours. That's what the relief workers keep telling you: You have to eat three meals a day. And you just keep doing as much as you can, and don't blame yourself for not doing more."

And if you are far away, and you cannot tote or ladle or dig or comfort small children, you still do what you can. And if you are lucky, you get to spend some time in the wilderness, away from television, lying on your back at night watching the canopy of constellations and thrilling at the shooting stars.

Fort Worth Star-Telegram
July 24, 1994

"We Were Wrong"—
This Time He's Right

> "We were wrong, terribly wrong. We owe it to future generations to explain why."
>
> —ROBERT S. McNAMARA,
> *former secretary of defense, speaking of the Vietnam War*

There it is. Thank you, Mr. McNamara.

"Stop the presses!" is the way we in the newspaper bidness say, "This is *really* important." I wish there were some way to stop all the presses—to get all the spin doctors and O.J. media hypesters and smug Republicans and backpedaling Democrats and busy moms and teens who only read about Madonna to sit down, be quiet, and listen to Robert McNamara for a little while.

Odd but appropriate that as we celebrate the fiftieth anniversary of our victory in the Good War, we should also be reminded of the one we mucked up. Important, so important, for everyone holding public office, everyone, to consider the possibility that twenty years hence they, too, may have to sit down and write: "We were wrong, terribly wrong."

And for those of us who were outside the Pentagon, on the other side of those fences and police lines, trying to scream truth to power, we, too, have something to learn from McNamara's confession.

Unless we understand how we got from the end of World War II— when we were the good guys, when we liked ourselves and stood for the right stuff, not to mention free chewing gum for foreign kids—to the end of the Vietnam War, then we cannot understand how we got from the end of 'Nam to where we are now. All this distrust and dislike that Americans now have for one another—all this cynicism. How did we get from raising the flag at Iwo Jima to My Lai?

No one person can wholly understand a tragedy like Vietnam, but I plan to put McNamara's book on the small shelf of indispensable books, along with Michael Herr's *Dispatches* and Neil Sheehan's *A Bright Shining Lie.* McNamara, ever the numbers-cruncher, offers us Reasons 1 Through 11, rather in the style of H&R Block, for why millions of people died in vain. Lying is one of them. Anything new? Wrong time + wrong place + wrong side = wrong war.

McNamara's subtitle is *Tragedy and Lessons of Vietnam.* Funny—people have been writing, and living, tragedies at least since the ancient Greeks, but are the lessons ever really new? The Greeks used to blame tragedy on hubris, the Greek word for a kind of poisonous pride, the pride of the just man who, because his intentions are noble, does not question himself or permit others to do so. In other languages there are separate words for good pride and bad pride (for example, in French, *fierte* and *orgueil*). McNamara painfully details all the times they could have listened, should have listened to those who disagreed.

What are we to learn, then, aside from the modest assessment I made years ago: You cannot prop up a government that does not have the support of its own people. McNamara concurs.

Part of the poison of Vietnam is that we ended it as badly as we fought it, and for that I blame Richard Nixon and Henry Kissinger. Lies, lies, lies, right through the end. It has taken us years, while the poison has spread, to lance the wound and let the pus out. By now we believe all politicians are liars. Last week in Washington, speaking to a group of journalists, I vigorously insisted that it is a far more important obligation of ours to root out official lies than it is to report on the private behavior of public officials. Came the question: "Do you really think lying is worse than adultery? Than breaking a vow made before God and company?"

I don't know. I do know that it ain't my job to know. All a journalist can do is cover the public realm; judgment of private lives is left to biographers, spouses, and God. In the public realm, lying is the original sin. And the only antidote for it is the truth told as unsparingly as Robert McNamara has done.

So our lessons are: Don't lie. Certitude is the enemy. Self-doubt is good. Particularly difficult lessons in a nervous age, when the search for certainty compels so many.

This column is dedicated to one of the 58,000-plus names on The Wall.

Fort Worth Star-Telegram
April 11, 1995

What I Did to Morris Udall

TUCSON, ARIZONA — Life's a funny ol' female-dog, idn't she? Here I am back in Tucson, one of my favorite places in the U.S. of A., and also the place of one of my most bitter professional regrets.

I did a man wrong here one time. I didn't mean to, and it didn't make much difference, but there it is. The man's name is Morris Udall, congressman from Tucson, and the year was 1976.

Six, I think it was, Democrats were scrapping for the presidential nomination that year. Ol' Gerry Ford looked beatable. Among the less likely contenders were Jimmy Carter, a former governor of Georgia with the charisma of a day-old pizza, and Mo Udall, an ace guy with the misfortune to be from Arizona (three electoral votes).

The New York Times Magazine was fixing to run profiles on each of these six candidates, and they called me to profile Udall—I think because I was the farthest-West journalist they'd ever heard of; Texas, Arizona—they all look the same from New York.

In those days I was what is known in our trade as "hungry," which is supposed to mean "feisty, ambitious, willin' to go after a story like a starvin' dog." Actually, I was plain hungry: Six years at the *Texas Observer* left me below the poverty line, and I jumped at that assignment.

So I came over to Arizona and investigated Mo Udall's life, times, finances, family life, psychological health, and public record back to Year Aught. I'll tell you now what I should have told you then: Udall is a man of exceptional decency, integrity, courage, honesty, and intelligence. On top of which, he's funny. If you could have forced Congress to take a vote back then just on the question of who was the finest human being then serving—secret ballot, no consequences, just vote your conscience—I swear to you that Udall would have won hands down.

And did I report this? No. I was looking for warts; I wanted dirt. Besides, I was afraid of being conned, of looking like a naïve hick. I dug through his campaign contributions. (I found union money! Do you know how brave you have to be to support unions in Arizona?) I dug through his psycho history (The Udalls are a famous Mormon family. Mo split from the church and became a Jack Mormon after commanding an all-black troop in the Army). I wrote about his being one-eyed. (At one point, he was a one-eyed professional basketball player—some handicap.)

Faced with the disgusting reality of a truly decent politician, I did my dead-level best to be tougher than a fifty-cent steak. I didn't cut him an inch of slack; I thought that was my job, the way they did it in the big leagues.

My grudging report that I hadn't been able to find anything actually wrong with Udall duly appeared in print. Imagine my surprise when *The New York Times*'s famed political correspondent R. W. Apple followed my reserved appraisal of Udall with a puff piece about Jimmy Carter. (Johnny Apple, you know perfectly well that was a puff piece.) Every venial sin of Udall's that I had held up to the merciless light of day, Apple glossed over gaily in the case of Carter. The profiles appeared from one Sunday to the next, but the politicians described in them were not judged by a single standard. To put it mildly.

Well, Jimmy Carter turned out to be a man of character and decency, too—he just wasn't much of a politician, and Mo Udall was a good one.

My continuing regret is that what I wrote was accurate, but it wasn't *true*. I was trying so hard to prove I could be a major-league, hard-hitting journalist that I let the real story go hang itself.

The real story is the sheer decency of Morris Udall. When I am asked if there are any heroes left in politics, I always think of Udall. He's retired now, victim of a sad, slow, wasting disease. I suppose you could say that Udall is to Arizona liberals what Barry Goldwater is to Arizona conservatives: an incurably honest man of principle. Or you could say that Morris Udall is to Arizona liberals what Ev Meacham is to Arizona kooks. I think he'd like to have it end with a joke.

Fort Worth Star-Telegram
June 12, 1994

Sex, Death, and Media Ethics

MINNEAPOLIS AND AUSTIN—What a mess. Famous people, divorce, suicide, scandalous allegations of sexual misconduct.

Got your attention, didn't I? And it gets better. After we get through wallowing in the gory details, then we get to self-righteously, and righteously, blame the media for bringing all this to our attention. Delicious, isn't it, Pecksniff, my dear?

Here's the deal. The first thing I need to do is disclose my own bias, since I have one. The late Michael Dorris—a fine and sensitive writer who most recently distinguished himself by tying a plastic bag over his head and snuffing out his life while registered under a false name at a New Hampshire motel—was a semifriend of mine. By that I mean that we admired each other's work, chortled over each other's stories, had dinner together a few times, and had in common a very dear friend.

This is going to be even worse than I thought when I first contemplated writing about it. But following LaMott's dictate that all you can do is be honest, the name of our mutual friend is Doug Foster. He has many other credentials, but so far he has figured in the public

prints on this story only as the "Douglas Foster of Berkeley, Calif.,"
who telephoned authorities in New Hampshire two weeks ago in time
to foil Michael's first attempt at suicide. Said authorities found Dorris
where Foster suspected he was hiding, pumped the pills, booze, and
applesauce out of him, and set him back on life's merry road—for a
brief time.

The proximate cause of Dorris's suicide is that he was in the midst
of a horribly painful divorce from his wife, Louise Erdrich, also a well-
known writer. The couple had lived not only in New Hampshire but
also in Minneapolis, where the local paper first printed the news of his
death directly underneath the obituary of an elderly woman who had
devoted her life to the cause of suicide prevention. I mention this in
part because I'm a sucker for irony, but also because it reminds me
that we, collectively, do know more about the causes of suicide, and
even some things about how to prevent it, than used to be the case.

In Dorris's case, I presume to doubt that much could have been
done. The man was not only in misery and despair, but his own father
had died a presumed suicide. Dorris's friends were fully aware of the
danger, calling across the country to warn one another: "He's gonna
kill himself, he's gonna kill himself—what can we do?"

After his first attempt, Dorris wound up briefly at a shrink farm.
Let us say only that there are varying opinions as to whether that experience was beneficial. They gave him a pass; he killed himself.

O.K., so now he's dead—what else is there to say? *Nil nisi bonum*
and all that, right? Nah. You underestimate your friendly media.

The Minneapolis *Star Tribune,* right there in the heart of Minnesota
Nice, needed to report that Dorris had been under investigation by
local authorities concerning "allegations of criminal sexual misconduct involving children."

"Possible criminal charges," "potential criminal charges." Pretty
sensational story, huh?

I mean, after all, as the *Strib* pointed out on its front page, "Dorris
was a nationally renowned advocate for children's welfare." Imagine

the hypocrisy of it: This guy who had written whole books, traveled around the country, preached about fetal alcohol syndrome until a girl who's pregnant feels like she can't even have a beer without endangering her child (according to Dorris, she can't)—imagine if this same guy is guilty of "criminal sexual misconduct with children." No wonder he offed himself, right?

Take a step back. Take two steps back. Let's stipulate, as the lawyers say, that the *Star Tribune* did a flawless job of reporting. Their reporter did just what they pay him to do: He got the story. Now the question is: Should you print it?

Two questions: (A) Is there any good reason to print this story? (B) Is there any good reason *not* to print this story?

(A) is easy: It's an incredible story.

(B)? You think we never ask that question? The classic answer to (B) is "troop movements in time of war." A few other examples from recent history: We (the media) knew that seven Americans had escaped from the U.S. Embassy during the Iranian hostage crisis and were hiding out elsewhere in Tehran, but we didn't print it, for obvious reasons. We knew that an American reporter was in Kuwait during the Iraqi occupation but didn't print it, for obvious reasons.

More recently we have been having a furious debate about whether *The Dallas Morning News* should have printed Tim McVeigh's alleged "confession" to the Oklahoma City bombing. Our rule is: If it's true and it's important, we go with it. No one pays us to sit on the news.

But we also go to these endless seminars on fair trial versus free press. We know perfectly well that if we print everything we know about certain criminal cases, the courts will determine that a fair trial is impossible, and the suspect will walk—right out of the courthouse, without even having to go through a trial. This was a real risk in the McVeigh case.

There are other examples of stuff we know but don't tell, but they tend to be local and to involve considerations of privacy. If a family wants the paper to report that their son died "after a lengthy illness" rather than "of AIDS complications," most papers won't push it. Don't ever ask us to lie, but we can avoid the full truth for all sorts of reasons.

So was there a good reason *not* to print allegations of sexual misconduct made against Michael Dorris—especially since he's safely dead? Some nitpickers might say it's unfair to print such allegations since there is no way to know whether they are true and no forum in which the truth can ever be established. Carpers.

We in the media don't have to prove that such charges are true before we print them; we only have to know that such charges are being made by duly constituted authorities—or at least that they would have been made, or that they *might* have been made, that they were possible or potential charges. So our standard of proof for smearing a dead man on page one is not real high. We've got the First Amendment, nyeh, nyeh, nyeh.

Dorris's lawyer, Doug Kelly of Minneapolis, used some legal terminology: "Decedants have rights, too." You couldn't prove that by the media.

But even by our own rather less-than-elevated standards, there's another consideration here. One of our odd reticences is that we do not, or at least we try not to, endanger the life of a child. It stems from old kidnapping cases, obviously going back to our miserable performance in the case of the Lindbergh baby. Our unofficial rule (we don't have any Official Rules) is that when the life of a child is at stake, We Should Attempt to Exercise Some Restraint. (As they used to say in East Texas, mighty white of us.) This usually means we shouldn't show up with our cameras at a designated drop-off for ransom or pull some other life-imperiling, deal-messing-up stunt.

In the case of Michael Dorris, now so publicly smeared as an alleged child molester, the problem is the child who made the allegation. Who thought about the kid? So far, the only one I've seen is Dorris's eighty-five-year-old mother, Mary. Her husband is long dead, now her only child is a suicide, and the first break in her composure came when the Minneapolis paper printed the allegation of child abuse.

"Don't they understand that Michael killed himself to prevent this from becomin' public?" she said. "Don't they understand that he did what he did so his family wouldn't be hurt? He thought if he did it, there wouldn't be nothin' in the papers, but now they've put it in anyway."

Now here's an odd note about media in our time: After the story about "possible criminal charges" against the defunct Dorris appeared, rumors began spreading via computer—specifically, a flood of E-mail from parties unknown, of unknown reliability—suggesting or even asserting all kinds of wild theories. Based on these reliable sources, reporters from bona fide, certified, legitimate news media began to call friends of Dorris, asking questions.

You take a call from a respectable wire service or newsmagazine and suddenly find yourself saying: "Yah, well, I knew him pretty well for twenty years, but I never saw any horns growing out of his head. . . . No, actually, never noticed a tail, either. . . . Gee, I wish I could help you, but he never tried to rape me. Had him up to my hotel room once, but all he did was talk about his wife and kids. . . . No, actually, I didn't try to rape him, either."

I don't know absolutely for sure that the allegations that have been made against Michael Dorris are untrue. But neither does anyone else know that they are true. I suppose it is possible that Dorris, who adored his own children and who fought so hard to help and protect and save other children, might have had some weird sexual kink of which his friends never got an inkling. Almost anything's possible. Senator Phil Gramm once invested in a porno movie.

All I am saying is that I think we should have thought far more carefully about the consequences of printing these allegations—far more carefully. Even beyond the privacy issue, the life of a child is at stake.

Fort Worth Star-Telegram
April 17, 1997

NOTE: This column was written shortly after the death of Michael Dorris, before newspapers broke the story that the allegation of child abuse came from Michael's own thirteen-year-old daughter, his eldest. This is the child I was trying to protect. The sensational charge touched off a wave of intensely negative stories about Dorris, including a notably careless one in *New York* magazine. Then, in a fine example of conscientious journalism, David Streitfeld of *The Washington Post* went back and looked very carefully indeed at the whole situation, not only correcting the many errors in earlier stories, but also presenting the evidence that made some of us doubt the credibility of Dorris's accusers from the beginning. Streitfeld found that Dorris's daughter had been seeing a therapist who works with "recovered memory" who was one of the leading figures in the infamous Jordan, Minnesota, scandal based on false recovered memory. The last line of Streitfeld's article is: "His three young daughters have been devastated by his death, particularly the eldest. She is said to be inconsolable."

Wasting Perfectly Good Anger

Perhaps what we need around here are lessons in how to get angry.

I grant you, the appeal of this notion is not immediately apparent. It would seem to the superficial observer that there is already a sufficiency of anger floating about in our great nation. Certainly the number of people who cannot talk about politics or the media or Wall Street or almost anything else without getting all red in the face is practically infinite. A more select group—the anger-gifted—turn purple; the tendons start to stand out in their necks, and their wattles commence to shake like a turkey gobbler's. Good grief.

It's not the quantity of anger in America that concerns me, or even the quality, but the sheer waste of anger. Yes, anger wastage is one of the little-noted problems in America.

The first problem is wasting anger on things that (A) don't exist at all or (B) matter so little that they might as well not exist. The U.N. plot to take over the world. Black helicopters. The international biosphere. The liberal media. (How long have those folks been out of the loop?) The Bilderbergers. The secular humanists. The cover-up of what happened to Flight 800. Al Gore's Red connections. (Got that from a recent edition of *The New American,* a veritable fountain of paranoia.) The plot to make America into a police state. And so forth.

Imagine wasting all that perfectly good anger on paranoid fantasies. Not since Emily Litella got upset about "Soviet jewelry" has there been such a waste of anger. You will notice a certain theme to these Emily Litella Moments. Behind them all is a touching faith that someone, somewhere, is actually in charge of what's happening—a proposition I beg leave to doubt.

In addition to inventing targets for anger, we suffer from the classic misdirection of anger. Misdirected anger, the shrinks tell us, is as common as dirt in family and human relationships. The most common pattern is when a big kid hits a little kid; the little kid can't hit the big kid back, so he goes and whacks a littler kid instead. You see it all the time. Guy is mad at his boss and can't do anything about it, so he comes home and yells at his wife and kids instead. And so on down the food chain.

Most of the racism you see is misdirected anger, from your basic Ku Klux Kluckers (who think black folks are somehow responsible for the way the world is run) to the folks who have decided that illegal immigrants are responsible for the decline of civilization (not to mention the American economy) to those Einsteins who have analyzed our problems and determined that teenage welfare mothers are behind the collapse of "values." The trouble with blaming powerless people is that although it's not nearly as scary as blaming the powerful, it does miss the point. Another Emily Litella Moment.

Poor people were not in charge of the S&Ls. Poor people do not shut down factories. Poor people are not in charge of those mergers and acquisitions in which tens of thousands of people lose their jobs so a few people in top positions can make a killing on the stock market. Poor people did not decide to keep wages either steady or falling for the last twenty years. Poor people didn't decide to use "contract employees" because they cost less and don't get any benefits.

You notice that the common corollary to blaming poor people for the country's problems is to blame poor people for their own problems. That's a particularly satisfying exercise, because if we can make ourselves believe that poor folks are responsible for their own problems, then the rest of us are absolved of any responsibility for them. Homeless people, people on welfare—hey, we know how to fix that: Those folks should just get a job, right? As though most people in poverty don't already have jobs.

The reason we like to blame the victim is because if it's not the victim's fault, why, then, it could happen to anybody. It could even happen to you. And that is scary. That's why we used to claim women got raped because they were in the wrong part of town, or were wearing short skirts, or should have known better than go into a bar, or to a fraternity party, or into an unlit parking lot, or out after dark, or . . . until women finally got fed up and said, "Forget that—let's blame the rapists instead."

People who blame the government for everything are at least closer to the power mark. But the sense of constriction for which so many of us blame the government—cutting the speed limit, making bikers wear helmets, telling us we can't put up a big sign on a building, can't add a garage without a permit, can't build a factory in a suburb, can't do this, can't do that, can't do the other—is not so much a reflection of a power-crazed government as it is of a crowded and complex society.

True, none of us are as free as we would have been had we lived on the frontier one hundred years ago. But this ain't a frontier, and this ain't one hundred years ago; the more crowded and complex society becomes, the more each of your actions is apt to impinge on someone around you. As Woodrow Call complained in *Lonesome Dove,* it's got so you can't even pee off your back porch anymore without upsetting the neighbors.

The amazing thing about what happens when you hold people with real power in this society responsible for the way it's run is that they, each and every one, will then begin to explain to you how powerless they are. My favorite example is "Chainsaw" Al Dunlap, the CEO who gets hired to fire people. Dunlap claims that he has no choice—he has to answer to those stockholders.

But I would suggest that you hold your fire, and your anger, for those who have power. Wasting it on imaginary threats or powerless people is wasting a valuable national resource.

Fort Worth Star-Telegram
May 6, 1997

We the People

Here's to a Nation
Undeterred by Reality

Happy Fourth, beloveds! As we celebrate our country's natal day, it's fun to catalogue some of the lovable stuff about America, an especially good idea this year, methinks, as we're all so grumpy with ourselves.

I'm a longtime fan of our national habit of polling ourselves to find out how dumb we are. ("Study Shows Americans Know Squat About . . ." geography, history, mathematics, our own Constitution— you name the subject, there's a study to show how ignorant we are about it. Then we all clap our hands to our foreheads and bemoan the national dumbness anew.) Just the other day a poll scientifically determined that we all think our morals are going to pot, too.

Personally, I like Americans. I think we're quite nice, on the whole. What you find when you get out and move about in this nation is that it's full of nice people, the news media to the contrary notwithstanding. Because the media focus so constantly on rapine, pillage, and murder, we tend to forget the remarkable number of swell folks hereabouts. So I say: Let's celebrate us.

The poet Marianne Moore once observed, "It is an honor to witness so much confusion," which is the way I feel about the whole joint.

Confronted with any given problem, Americans can be counted upon to promptly mount horse and gallop off in 360 different directions. This is far more interesting than living in Canada, where the national motto is, "Now, let's *not* get excited."

Who, me? Generalize? I love the terminal practicality of Midwesterners, the dotty charm of Southerners, and the *yeee-hah!* exuberance of Texans. I love smart-mouthed New Yorkers, parsimonious Yankees, and blue-haired ladies in Florida who put rhinestone collars on their miniature poodles.

For some reason, many people believe that England is the great nation for eccentrics; this is because they see nothing peculiar about all the Americans who have dedicated their lives to setting a world record for knocking over dominoes in sequence. Or crocheting toilet-paper covers. Or collecting Fiesta ware. Of course, this means that our teenagers have to dye their hair blue, green, or orange in order to be considered odd, but what the hey, it adds color to the streets.

We're the country that put Elvis on a stamp! We buy pink lemonade and striped toothpaste! Sixty-seven point two percent of us believe that Alexis de Tocqueville never should have divorced Blake Carrington! Huge numbers of us believe in flying saucers, horoscopes, palm readers, the lottery, pyramid power, that John Kennedy was killed by the CIA, and that you can get AIDS off toilet seats. A nation undeterred by reality—no wonder we went to the moon!

Consider American cuisine: pizza, kung pao chicken, sushi, tacos, bratwurst, tofu burgers, and corn on the cob. Who wants to live in a place that favors unanimity and uniformity? Consider American music: jazz, blues, pop, country, folk, opera, heavy-metal rock, Cajun, polka, Gershwin, Sousa, bluegrass, Tejano, baroque, Cole Porter, punk, Latino, industrial rock, Three Tenors, reggae, and . . . what have I left out? This is not a case of thirty-seven flavors of the same thing, which is more than anyone needs—this is about *possibility*.

O.K., O.K., so America is not what you could consider a highly tasteful country. So we can do better than Barbie and the Golden

Arches. One thing you can count on is that we will. Maybe our national motto should be, "You want it, we got it."

I grant you, the USA requires a considerable tolerance for diversity and a fondness for dissent. The full-throated roar of a free people exercising their constitutional right to free speech can be a little deafening at times. But peace and quiet and solitude are among our options. This is the country with Enough Room. If you don't believe it, go to Lubbock.

So here's a Glorious Fourth to all y'all certified Good Folks. The ones who stop to help the ones who have flat tires; the ones who return the wallets and recycle the cans and bottles; the ones who mean it when they say, "Have a nice day"; and the ones who observe wryly, "If it was a snake, it woulda bit you." Here's to the Americans who make pickle relish and give it to their neighbors, who pick up trash on Clean the Beaches Day and other times, who chat with strangers to be friendly, and who make waitresses laugh. Happy Fourth.

Fort Worth Star-Telegram
July 4, 1995

This Is a Great Nation

Happy birthday to us! No shortage of material for a Fourth of July column celebrating the nuttiness, diversity, and rampageous, outsize je ne sais quoi (as we always say in Lubbock) that makes these shores such a treat to live on.

You must admit that we have more interesting heavyweight championship boxing matches than the average place. And a charitable organization has demonstrated our extreme flexibility by naming Rupert Murdoch "Humanitarian of the Year," an award that was presented by Henry Kissinger.

We live in a great nation.

On this, the eve of our 221st natal date, the economy is rocking along. True, the rising tide is lifting the yachts a lot faster than the rowboats, but it still beats a stick in the eye, so we might as well celebrate. Crime is down, school scores are up here, and there is no baseball strike this year.

We know that free speech is in good shape—not only because the Supremes just came thumping out with a big decision that applies the First Amendment to cyberspace, but also because kvetching is the national pastime. Our public scolds are in rare plumage and regularly inform us that our morals have gone to pieces, our families are falling apart, our society is the most decadent since the palmy days of the late Roman empire, our kids are spoiled rotten, and our government can't do anything right. In order to correct all this, they advocate a constitutional amendment against flag-burning.

We live in a great nation.

We're still a little confused about sex, of course, as befits descendants of Puritans. At least we're providing amusement for other nations in this regard. The president is being sued on grounds of sexual harassment, and the Air Force has achieved such an advanced state of dingbattery on matters sexual that it had to retreat to the safer ground of denying that space aliens have been landing near Roswell, New Mexico. Of course, no one believed them.

The Walt Disney Company, creator of adorable cartoon critters beloved by children everywhere, is now being boycotted by the Southern Baptists as a sink of perversion. Now, there's an interesting development.

Our latest fad is the cabbage diet, which raises the always timely question: Is God punishing us?

Our democracy is under a slight cloud, but fear not: with Ol' Ethics-Fine Gingrich at the helm and that saintly fellow Representative Dan Burton fixing to investigate how other people raise campaign money, we can look forward to a high level of entertainment provided by the public purse in the near future.

This is a great nation.

The thing about democracy, beloveds, is that it is *not* neat, orderly, or quiet. It requires a certain relish for confusion. So let us repair to the purple mountain majesties, the shining shores, or the backyard, there to tuck into our fried chicken, hot dogs, corn on the cob, potato salad, ice cream, fireworks, and John Philip Sousa. Or, as the case may be, arugula, radicchio, confit of duck with gingered figs, shiitake mushrooms, sorrel salad, raspberry purée, fireworks, and John Philip Sousa.

And as we wish our country happy birthday, endeavor to recall two things: (1) Most Americans really are much nicer people than we often give ourselves credit for being; and (2) "the pursuit of happiness" was an eighteenth-century locution for "the search for justice and right."

Besides, next year, someone else will be Humanitarian of the Year, and with any luck, it won't be O. J. Simpson. Have a glorious Fourth.

Fort Worth Star-Telegram
July 3, 1997

Look Out, News Fans! Here Comes August

Great, the country is about to gain a budget and lose St. Louis, and August is only two days old.

You know how satisfying it is when somebody comes up with evidence to support a pet theory of yours? Well, someone has finally done it for one of my pet theories, which is that August is a terrific month.

Of course, you have to factor in here that I'm in the newspaper business, where we thrive on strife, disaster, conflict, the weird, the astonishing, and the absurd. It took the newspaper business to contribute the phrase "a good murder" to the language.

"Never take a vacation in August," I tell young reporters, "because it's so easy to get on the front page." August is just one great news story after another, and besides, it's when the editors usually take their vacations.

But even in our business you will find doubters who claim that the dread dog days are also slow news days. Piffle. I now have corroborating evidence from a gent named Bruce Handy, writing in *The New York Times Magazine,* that August is, just as I always suspected, a pip of a news month. Chock full of one juicy, amazing event after another.

Just because people are a little grumpy from the heat is no reason not to relish the confusion.

As Handy points out, even President Bush, in one of his rare diagrammable sentences, once inquired, "What is it about August?" That was after the second year in a row during which his annual attempt to retreat to Kennebunkport had been disrupted by crisis (Iraq invaded in Kuwait in '90, and the Soviet coup occurred in August '91).

War, riot, disaster, assassination—what a festival of news we have every year during the eighth month—and always some good murders, too.

In my own twenty-five years of covering August nuttiness, I drew the assignment that may yet prove to be my greatest claim to being a Witness to History—at least it's the one that most impresses people I meet buying the *National Enquirer* in the grocery-store checkout line: I covered Elvis Presley's funeral. He's definitely dead.

That fateful August 16, I was working for the aforementioned *New York Times*, a paper that follows the Boy Scout motto, "Be Prepared," and thus has an extensive obituary desk, usually ready to go with an obit of any prominent person who might croak.

But Elvis, you recall, died untimely. The *Times* was not prepared. A sort of grave, stately *Times*ian panic ensued. The paper has music critics by the note-load: classical, opera, modern, jazz, even rock. But it just wasn't the kind of paper where Elvis fans worked. Except for me. They knew I was one 'cause I have this funny accent.

So I wrote Elvis's obit for *The New York Times*, following the in-this-case bizarre *Times* practice of referring to him throughout as "Mr. Presley." The next day we sold more papers than we had since John Kennedy was shot, and the *Times* decided to send me to Memphis for the obsequies.

I arrive late, already close to deadline, jump in a cab, and holler, "Take me to Graceland!" The cabbie peels out of the airport doing eighty and then turns full around to the backseat and drawls, "Ain't it a shame Elvis had to die while the Shriners are in town?"

And so they were, the place was crawling with them, and you know Shriners in convention, wearin' they l'il red fezzes, ridin' up and down the hotel hallways on they tricycles, tootin' those New Year's Eve horns. Every hotel in Memphis was crammed with Shriners, and on top of that, ten thousand grieving, hysterical Elvis fans show up.

There was no room at any inn, Holiday or otherwise, so the Memphis Chamber arranged to put the visiting press corps up in a dormitory at Memphis State College. I didn't get out there until near midnight, dead tired after last deadline, only to see, through the plate-glass doors of the dorm, many young people bouncing up and down while screaming, "Pizza man, pizza man; rah, rah, rah."

Naturally I assumed I was hallucinating. But no. Also taking place that very week on the Memphis State campus was what was billed as the World's Largest Cheerleading Camp. Don't know if you know much about cheerleading camp, but the object is for your cheerleadin' team to win the Spirit Stick, which looks, to the uninitiated eye, a whole lot like a broom handle painted red, white, and blue. But it is the Spirit Stick. And if your team wins it for three days in a row, you get to keep it, but that has never happened. The way you win the Spirit Stick is by showing the Most Spirit. The way you show spirit is you bound out of bed in the morning, do handstands end-over-end down the hall to the john, cheer while brushin' your teeth, cheer while washin' your face, cheer for breakfast, lunch, and dinner, and when the pizza man brings the pizza.

For three days I interviewed grieving, hysterical Elvis fans while tripping over Shriners ridin' tricycles while tootin' those New Year's Eve horns, and then I went back to this dormful of young people, determined to out-spirit one another.

And none of it surprised me.

Because I know from August.

Fort Worth Star-Telegram
August 3, 1993

Fire and Flakiness
on the West Coast

LOS ANGELES—Poor LA-LA Land: edgy, fearful, prone to flights of apocalyptic fancy. The radio announcer intones, "And the fires are sweeping down toward . . ."

"Fires? What fires? Where are the fires? Is it . . . ?"

No, it's not. It's just the usual Southern California dry-season brushfires. Arson, of course, is suspected.

Weird rumors float: The blacks have already started killing cops. They're gonna kill one a day. The newspapers know this, but they won't print it.

I mildly suggest, based on twenty-five years' experience in the newspaper trade, that there is no such thing as a good story that a newspaper won't print. It makes no impact. Everyone here believes some strange, off-kilter version of reality. Gossip, rumor, and urban myth, conspiracy theorists on the radio call-in shows lending credence to dark and sinister views. Maybe nothing is too weird to believe since the Manson killings. Maybe it has always been harder to tell fact from myth in Tinseltown.

No more California dreamin', no more wishing they all could be

California girls, no more laid-back, mellow, golden California. They pick obsessively at the sores: the Rodney King verdict, the Reginald Denny verdict. Two wrongs don't make a right, they all agree. But there is some level on which they are pleased that it balanced in the end. Two terrible verdicts—and a secret sense of relief.

Legal scholars are appalled: What did the Denny jury do? Establish riot as a defense against misconduct? Is it O.K. to pound someone in the head with a brick because there's a riot going on? Professor Paul Robinson, writing in *The Wall Street Journal,* asks: "But do we want to live in a world where criminal trials are decided by the politics of the day? That is a mad dog that may bite your enemy today but you tomorrow. If these acquittals avoid a riot now, they plant seeds for many in the future."

Maybe. But in L.A., one keeps finding that hidden sense of relief, the notion that somehow the two bad verdicts canceled each other out, that some rough equivalence of justice was achieved. You have to be badly frightened to turn ancient, inherited wisdom on its head, to believe two wrongs do make a right.

But Southern California being Southern California, it can't even approach anarchy and apocalypse without its own special form of nuttiness intervening. Right after the Denny verdict came down, Gloria Allred, the feminist lawyer, was doing her radio talk show (very few people in Los Angeles do *not* have a radio talk show) and discussing the verdict with the head of the public defender's office. In the middle of this heavyweight legal discussion, Allred gets a call from Heidi Fleiss, the Hollywood Madam, who is calling in regards to an earlier talk show on which she was criticized by an earlier guest. So Allred puts the legal maven on hold to chat with Fleiss: the Hollywood Madam is *very, very* UPSET about having been criticized, and although it's true that it wasn't on Allred's show or by Allred's guest, she is still *very* upset, and so Allred begins to counsel her in this wonderful California fashion.

She, Heidi, says Allred, is going through a very stressful time and must remember to take care of herself. Now, what is she doing for her mental health, for her inner child? Is she taking massage? And she must do something to take her mind off her legal problems.

Oh! replies the Hollywood Madam, indeed she does have a new interest in life. In fact, she's putting out a new line of designer pajamas. Whereupon, Fleiss, the Hollywood Madam, and Allred, the feminist lawyer, begin discussing the new line of designer pajamas, and possibly other lingerie as well. All while the legal eagle waits on hold to continue talking about whether the verdict in the Denny case will touch off a new race riot. After the pajama discussion has ended, other listeners call in to announce they are planning to buy automatic weapons, because, really, it's just the *only* way to feel safe in this town anymore, and by the way, they can't *wait* to see the new line of pajamas.

Today the sky is raining ashes on downtown L.A. from all the brushfires in the area, so the sense of Apocalypse Now is still strong. But even if rain should come to put out the brushfires, it will only cause massive mudslides that destroy more homes, so, thinks the Angeleno, there is not that much point in worrying about it, and has anyone seen the Hollywood Madam's new pajama line?

Los Angeles may indeed be on the verge of some massive social implosion, but if it goes, it's gonna go with a *lot* of je ne sais quoi.

Fort Worth Star-Telegram
October 28, 1993

The Pea and the Shell

Living, as we do, in a nation plagued by skater-on-skater violence, it is not easy for us to keep our collective eye on the shell with the pea under it.

No sooner does a body get to noodling around with a headline like U.S. MOVES TO HALT S&L SALES AMID CONCERN ON INSIDERS' PROFIT than in comes the verdict on Lorena Bobbitt, which, let's face it, does call for at least a moment's pause for reflection on the relationship between our criminal-justice system and the fate of John Wayne Bobbitt's male organ.

Just as I was fixing to become seriously exercised over the several idiocies buried in the Senate version of the crime bill, Dan Quayle appeared in a Wavy Lay's potato-chip commercial during halftime of the Super Bowl.

Any fool can tell Quayle's appearance in the Wavy Lay's commercial is Significant, but the more difficult question is, *what* does it signify? I suspect it will prove to be useful evidence for future Ph.D. thesis writers trying to plot the downward trajectory that follows the obligatory fifteen minutes of fame.

Next, following Sherlock Holmes's famous dictum concerning the significance of the dog that did *not* bark in the night, I was on the trail of a stunning insight concerning the neglect of basic Keynesian economics in our time, and the consequences of that neglect, when Tonya Harding's ex-husband grassed on her.

Don't talk to me about priorities, I was raised in the newspaper bidness and I know a good story when I see one. Skater-on-skater violence meets all the criteria: it's new, it's different, and while it may not be directly relevant to our lives, it's a lot easier to understand than why Serbs kill Bosnians.

Operating on the theory that if you've got lemons, you should make lemonade, I set out to prove with a ruler and compass that American newspapers have actually devoted more column inches to Michael Jackson's possible pedophilia than they have to the S&L scandal in toto, 1981 through 1994.

I was also busy with the Bobbitts' induction ceremony into the White Trash Hall of Fame.

Since I am a card-carrying intellectual, I subscribe to *The New York Review of Books,* which I count on to raise my eyes from tawdry quotidian ephemera up to the more lasting questions about who slept with whom in the Bloomsbury group. I believe the *NYRB* did once print instructions on how to make a Molotov cocktail, but that was in the 1960s, when many people lost their sense of proportion. It has since been reliably concerned only with Flaubert's concept of Art and with Freudian splinter groups. The new *New York Review of Books* has just arrived with a cover article on the Menendez case by Elizabeth Hardwick. You may well ask, "Why?" And I tell you it is because they couldn't get Joseph Brodsky to cover the Bud Bowl.

According to Flaubert's concept of Art, Tonya Harding should shortly begin dating Lyle Menendez. But since the world is now being scripted by Geraldo Rivera rather than Flaubert, Lorena Bobbitt will soon be dating William Kennedy Smith after they meet on Sally Jessy Raphaël's show.

Still in pursuit of my theory that the shrinking of the middle class portends something or other, I was reading a book on economic theory when I was interrupted by the crisis over Snoop Doggy Dogg's First Amendment rights. Mr. Dogg, as *The New York Times* so nicely puts it, is a practitioner of gangster rap, which, also according to the *Times,* is largely an indictment of bourgeois black cultural and political institutions by young people who do not find conventional methods of addressing personal and social calamity useful. Or, in the elegant phraseology of Mr. Dogg, "Fuck this fucking fucker, it's fucked."

Mr. Dogg's appearance in a Wavy Lay's potato-chip commercial caused me to lose sight of the pea completely, and the shells too, for that matter, which is why I'm giving up for now. I'll be back next month to try again.

The Progressive
March 1994

My, Oh, My, It's the Ninth Wonder of the World

MALL OF AMERICA, MINNESOTA — Great Caesar's armpit! Sweet suffering catfish! Holy gamoley! I have been to the Pyramids of America. I have seen the cathedral of commerce. Our Parthenon, our Coliseum, our Chartres. I have been to the Mall of America, the world's largest shopping mall.

To the archaeologists of the future, this sumbitch will rival Stonehenge and the mystery of the Easter Island heads. In the middle of the Nation's Largest Shopping Mall is Camp Snoopy, a combination carnival and Disneyland based on the oeuvre of Charles Schulz. Somewhere in it, a large cartoon of Snoopy thinks in balloon. "Good grief!" Let me second that motion.

Once before in my life I have had exactly the same feeling that the Mall of America gave me: the occasion in upstate New York when I was privileged to see a thousand-pound cheese go by in a parade. "My," I thought, "that certainly is something!" There are many wonders in our great nation.

The Mall of America presents the student of America with several conundrums. One: Just because this is the biggest, is it actually different from other shopping areas? Aside from the fact that there are carnival rides in the middle of it, is it different from the Riverwalk in San Antonio, which has a river in it, or the Galleria in Houston, which has an ice-skating rink in it? Well, yes. But it's like the difference between a five-hundred-pound cheese and a thousand-pound cheese. Certainly something, but not as impressive as it would be if you had only ever seen a two-pound cheese before.

Best specialty-shoppe name in the mall: Maison du Popcorn.

Of course I came prepared to dislike the Mall of America: I'm an intellectual and consequently obliged to despise popular culture in order to demonstrate my own good taste. But I have the same problem with the Mall of America that I have with Las Vegas, another place I was prepared to loathe on grounds of taste. I am an incurable and rather indiscriminate liker of people. Plunked someplace where I can watch people being themselves, I am a happy camper. Of course it would be better if it were the Café des Flores in Paris or the Café du Monde in New Orleans or the Angel Lodge at the Grand Canyon. But given a very large shopping mall, I have a dandy time.

I have come to love Las Vegas on the grounds that it is so tacky it is an art form in itself—haute tacky. The Mall of America has nothing like the gaudy, impudent glitz of Vegas—that in-your-face elevation of the rhinestone over the diamond—but in its johns-are-sanitized-for-your-protection way, the Mall of America is also an art form. It is haute nice.

I must confess to a secret prejudice here: I have long thought that Minnesotans are the nicest people in America. I know they hate that stereotype: I'm really sorry. But they are awfully nice. One local told me that she liked to go to the Mall of America because of the amazing variety of people there—people come from Latin America to the airport and go straight to the mall! she said. Teenage gangs hang out there! You see people of color!

All of this is true, but they are Latins in Minnesota, they are Minnesota gang members, they are Minnesota people of color. You may not believe this, but it is gospel: I once rode, for journalistic purposes, with the Minnesota Hell's Angels. They're awfully nice people.

Despite what passes in Minnesota for a polyglot crowd, the Mall of America is one of the whitest places I've ever been. Enough so to make a Texan uncomfortable, not to mention an Angeleno or Atlantan.

Nice is a pallid virtue. Not like honesty or courage or perseverance. On the other hand, in a nation frequently lacking in civility, there is much to be said for nice.

A note: It is great fun to watch children having fun. In our culture, little children are permitted wonder, but teenagers are not. Poor teens are always having to go around being cool—such a burden, no delight permitted. The only thing I saw at the Mall of America that reduced teenagers to wonder was the Wildlife Show, a talking parrot named Norman, a slightly confused ferret, and an impressive boa constrictor. Perhaps we are raising a generation that is inured to the wonders wrought by man and can be impressed only by nature.

And what are we, the spiritual descendants of Puritans, to make of this monument to materialism? So much stuff it makes you sick to look at it, like eating too much cotton candy. Stores that sell only stuff to put your stuff in. Subspecialties of stuff beyond the wildest dreams of most of the world's people. Should we not disapprove? Well, yeah. On the other hand, the Pyramids were built for pharaohs on the happy theory that they could take their stuff with them. Versailles was built for kings on the theory that they should live surrounded by the finest stuff. The Mall of America is built on the premise that we should all be able to afford this stuff. It may be a shallow culture, but it's by-God democratic. Sneer if you dare; this is something new in world history.

Fort Worth Star-Telegram
May 15, 1994

Sausage, Streets, Zoning—
Only in Chicago

CHICAGO—Finding myself in Chicago with a few hours free, I naturally took a busman's holiday and went to see the City Council in action. For political junkies like myself, going to the Chicago City Council is like going to Lourdes. O sacred source of endless, wonderful stories; O fabulous Pinkie Ring City.

I arrive just in time to hear the difficult matter of Andy's Deli and Mikolajczyk (sausage shop) go before the zoning committee. As all you attentive citizens know, zoning fights are the very guts of government, where we see the interests of one party come into conflict with the interests of another, thus resulting in knotty conflict to be settled through the collected wisdom of the ages in the form of the zoning process. It is, in its way, a majestic thing to witness.

The situation is this: Andy's Deli and Mikolajczyk is on the corner of Hermitage and Division, Hermitage being a residential street and Division a main stem. Andy's neighbors on Hermitage complain that the trucks serving his sausage plant—which employs fifty-six people—let us not forget that—are always snarling up the street, plus there's awful (I believe this is Chicagoan for *offal*) in the alley, plus Andy now proposes some kind of expansion that the neighbors are unclear about but which could make things a lot worse.

Andy, with his sausage empire on the line, his livelihood at stake, his day of decision arrived, has dressed for the occasion in a black-and-white checked shirt, plus his purple jacket with the purple slacks that do not match. Andy brings with him one neighbor, a nice lady with white hair, who says that Andy is a good guy and that she has never been bothered by the sausage operation. Andy says he proposes to take care of his neighbors' complaints by building a one-story garage that will hold all the trucks so they will not block the street, plus it would be good if the city were to make a cul-de-sac on the last block of Hermitage before Division Street by putting a curb across the street so nobody would bother anybody.

Right away, all the cognoscenti in my part of the gallery announce that the fix is in, which I do not see, being new to Chicago politics. They explain they know this because the alderman is at Andy's side.

Then the neighbors, all two of them, get their go and they have with them the ward committeeman, who is a woman (no PC in the Chicago City Council). They explain that a neighborhood meeting concerning the problems presented by the *mikolajczyk* was to have been held in the nearby Czar Bar, but no sooner had it gotten started than *some people* (heavy glances of suspicion here aimed at Andy and party) insisted that the Czar Bar was too hot, and so they all repaired across the street to the Bop Shop instead, and who knows how many confused citizens might have shown up at the Czar Bar looking for the meeting that they did not know was across the street, and this is the reason for the low turnout of anti*mikolajczyk* neighbors.

Andy's side at once ripostes that the temperatures in the Czar Bar were such as to make the room uncomfortable for senior citizens and that they resent the implication of foul play. The matter teeters back and forth before the concerned members of the City Council's zoning committee (only one of whom was sound asleep, although several sported arresting combinations of polyester). The neighbors make a gaffe when they mention that part of their problem is that they don't even know what ward they're in anymore, so how can they know who to go to about this? This unfortunate reference to what seems to be a grievous problem in drawing aldermanic lines offends the presiding councilman, who takes it as something of a slap at the majesty of the council that it doesn't even know where the ward lines are.

This might have been a fatal blow against the neighbors' case, except that the alderman himself, not taking sufficient notice of the chairman's sense of offense, also mentions that he has been handling this problem although he isn't sure these people are even in his district—and would we please not forget that Andy employs fifty-six people.

At this point, the smart money in the gallery is all on Andy's side. I am siding with the neighbors on the grounds that this is a case of the People against Big Capital, but the most I hope for is postponement; in my experience, zoning boards mostly postpone.

At this point, the zoning department is called upon and from the files retrieves the information that Andy was cited a few years ago for operating a more-than-15-percent retail (or maybe it was wholesale) business without the proper zoning and that his plans for the garage, et cetera, are not an expansion but an effort to get his shop in compliance with existing zoning. This puts quite a different complexion on the alleged expansion and leads, naturally, to the committee voting to postpone the decision, to my satisfaction.

I later repair to the *mikolajczyk* itself, where I find Andy, still in purple jacket, peacefully retailing (but not more than 15 percent of his total sausage output) *zwykla, kabanosy, krakowska, zywieka, kujawska,* and other, less recognizable forms of sausage. He says that the fight is over and that only one neighbor was against him anyway. True, I see a truck blocking Hermitage, but Andy is so genial and his sausage so good that I abandon the populist cause of the neighbors in favor of the beleaguered small businessman and decide what this country needs is more entrepreneurs like Andy. Also, the cul-de-sac is not a bad idea.

The next morning I awake in another city to find dulcimer music playing on the NPR station, and then the news comes on and the lead item is that the symphony orchestra is going on strike. "I must be back in Minnesota," I cried. And so I was.

Fort Worth Star-Telegram
October 11, 1994

The Zaniness of Texas Not Enough? Try New Mexico

SANTA FE, N.M. — The pluperfectly daffy charm of New Mexico's politics is in full and glorious display here in the early spring, bursting forth in such zany abundance that the New Mexico political fan can scarcely count all the blessings.

The Lege is in emergency session in the Roundhouse (that's the state capitol) trying to deal with a most unfortunate loophole in the state gas law that it wrote. It seems the law permits Indian tribes to sell gasoline wholesale all over the state, tax-free, with an unhappy impact on the state treasury. The Indians are industriously doing so, thus making Republican Governor Gary Johnson unhappy enough to call this rather expensive special session.

Meanwhile, Indians from the Pojoaque pueblo are out fouling up traffic on a major state highway because of a snafu of another sort. Casino gambling is a rich new source of Indian revenue all over the country, and New Mexico Indians are naturally cashing in. (Around the country, Indians are calling casino gambling "the new buffalo.") Johnson signed a gambling agreement with the tribes that has since been declared illegal by the state supreme court, so the casinos are in legal limbo. Johnson refused to put the issue on the agenda for the special session, thus touching off the Pojoaque traffic protest.

Tribal governor Jacob Viarrial says that if the state takes away the gambling revenue, his pueblo will put up tollbooths on the highway that crosses tribal land to make up for it. Now, if one were to step back here and take the long, long view, the prospect of American Indians becoming filthy rich from the stupidity of European-Americans who gamble does constitute a certain—hmmmm, what is the word we want here?—justice. But the long view is ever hard to maintain, and the motorists who were delayed for up to two hours Thursday lost it entirely.

Meanwhile, Santa Fe—which is now challenging Boulder, Colorado, for the title of Alfalfa Sprout Capital of the Universe—is also in a political pickle. Mayor Debbie Jaramillo was elected two years ago as a reform candidate, but she then proceeded to raise some nasty doubts about her purity by appointing her brother the city manager. Her brother then appointed her brother-in-law the chief of police. Nepotism is an old bane in New Mexico politics.

Just as the City Council was voting to fire the brother, Jaramillo received an international award for making Santa Fe a "city of vision," thus completing the confusion. Jaramillo denounced one of the council members who voted against her brother for having "just got off the bus." This set an alarming number of sensitivities jangling, since the native population of northern New Mexico consists of all the Hispanics, all the Indians, and about seven Anglos. Some Anglos who have lived here for fifty or sixty years are grudgingly accorded the status of full New Mexicans, but the interlopers of a mere ten or twenty years' standing are still regarded with suspicion.

In the old days, the division of power in New Mexico was beautifully simple: The Hispanics had the political power, the Indians had the federal government, and the Anglos had the money. All were united in their loathing of Texans, who are, of course, loud, vulgar, and rich. Happily for Texans, we have since been supplanted in general loathing by Californians, who are flooding into this very poor state with such buckets of money that Texans seem genteel by comparison.

Northern New Mexico is one of those places so ridiculously beautiful that the minute newcomers step aboard, they want to pull up the gangplank so more people won't come and spoil it. Your basic environmentalist-versus-developer wars here are aggravated by the extremely fragile, arid ecology. Although Santa Fe is now hopelessly condemned to be a tourist town, quainted up to the nines, it stubbornly refuses to build an airport, thus saving itself from becoming Disneyland-on-the-Sangre de Christos.

The cultural wars are also lively. The Indians have money to put into politics, the New Agers have introduced crystals and massage, the Hispanics-who-are-*not*-Chicanos are still struggling to preserve their culture, and the most unwelcome California import is gang warfare in Albuquerque. (It is evident to all devout New Mexicans that gang warfare comes from California; obviously, New Mexico kids would never have thought up gang wars on their own.)

Although Texas naturally wishes our wonderful neighbors the best of luck in solving all these problems, for the outsider the simplest way to understand politics here remains to heed a saying of my favorite former New Mexico governor, Bruce King: "A promise is not a commitment."

Fort Worth Star-Telegram
March 24, 1996

Alaska: Hope It Doesn't Get Messed Up

ANCHORAGE — Alaska is fabulous! People have been telling me that for years, and I always said: Yeah, sure, I'll get there someday. And now that I have, like any convert, I want to proselytize madly.

Alaska is so beautiful, so big, so funny, so amazing! It's full of all these astonishing Animatronic animals, and whenever a tour guide pushes a button, eagles swoop down to catch fish, whales spout and breach, and sea otters pop up cradling their babies on their breasts. And all the unemployed Alaskans are paid to wander around the woods in bear suits in the summertime to thrill the tourists. It's *much* better than Disneyland. And they accept American currency.

Alaskans themselves are charming, fluent in English and quite patient with tourists. They seem to regard us as a species of musk ox (a primitive bovine with a brain the size of a walnut) and calmly counsel us not to stand under calving glaciers or feed ham sandwiches to the grizzly bears. It's scarcely dangerous at all, although I was severely mauled by an attack crab. Later I ate it, with great satisfaction.

There are fortunes to be made here. For example, many Alaskans love to garden, but they have a hard time keeping moose out of their gardens. Keeping a moose from doing whatever it wants, including chowing down on your romaine and arugula, is notoriously difficult. One thing that works is spraying wolf pee around your garden. Naturally, some enterprising Alaskan is already selling wolf pee at forty dollars a quart. But no one has yet thought of selling free-range wolf pee, milked from wolves in the wild, so superior to mere domestic wolf pee. We're thinking of calling our free-range pee Moose-Away, or perhaps Vamoose.

Alaska is so wild, beautiful, and pure, so like the American West of fifty or one hundred years ago—except for a thin veneer of franchise restaurants, yogurt shops, and T-shirt stands—that one's protective instincts come out immediately. One wants to plead, "Please, puhleeze, don't screw this up the way we did our states." Alaskans, quite naturally, are not interested in advice from Lower 48ers about how to manage their resources. An independent (not to say slightly cussedminded) lot, they resent the federal gummint, environmentalists, and other forms of bossy do-gooders who tell them how many fish they can catch, crabs they can pot, seals they can shoot, and so forth.

Their legislature, on which I have impeccable sources, is a collection of greed-heads, gazooneys, and garbanzo-brains that would be a credit to Texas. And their congressional delegation! Their only representative, Don Young, once said: "Perseverance will overcome intelligence every time, and I'm going to stick to it." This guy makes Steve Stockman look like Albert Einstein. I have a strong sympathy for Alaskans' aversion to being told what to do and not do, except for this one thing. The worst case of environmental rape in America is being conducted on our nickel: Tax dollars from the Lower 48 are subsidizing something that would be a disgrace in a Third World country.

The Tongass National Forest is the last temperate rain forest left in North America. Unfortunately, it's under a fifty-year logging contract to Ketchikan Pulp Company, a subsidiary of the giant, multinational Louisiana-Pacific Corporation. The contract, which runs until 2004, was made when Alaska was desperate for industry and had nothing to offer but its natural resources. The contract stank then, and it reeks now, and Louisiana-Pacific actually has the nerve to ask for a fifteen-year extension on the contract—and has the support of Alaska's delegation. Louisiana-Pacific is paying well below market value (as recently as a few years ago, many estimated they were paying as low as $1.45 a tree; this included five-hundred-year-old Sitka spruce, which could be modified and sold straight to the Pacific Rim countries) while the taxpayers are footing the bill to the tune of $102 million over three years, according to a 1995 General Accounting Office report.

Now, get this: Alaska's Senator Frank Murkowski, who introduced the bill for the fifteen-year extension, owned between $15,000 and $50,000 worth of stock in Louisiana-Pacific until publicity forced him to sell it last year. He also owns stock valued at more than $1 million in the First Bank of Ketchikan and received between $50,000 and $100,000 in dividends from the bank in 1994. As Mr. Rogers would ask, "Can you say 'conflict of interest,' children?"

There is much more to this amazing tale. There's something about a frontier that seems to make corporations revert to their robber-baron instincts. Exxon and Louisiana-Pacific are just two of the most notable. More true tales of life on the wild frontier coming soon. Just remember, folks: You're paying for them.

Fort Worth Star-Telegram
June 25, 1996

Berkeley: It Is Its Own Place, but I'm Coming Home

BERKELEY, CALIFORNIA — "Ah," said my wise friend Deirdre, "you are going to write one of those articles about 'Berserkeley.' "

Nah—at least I hope not. On the other hand, you cannot expect me to resist the lunatic comedy of the place. Honest, there's a "Mexican restaurant" here that serves quesadillas with "duck, shiitake mushrooms, braised fennel, and eggplant" on that well-known Mexican specialty, the sun-dried tomato tortilla.

One night at a yuppie restaurant, I was faced with a choice between "sun-dried tomato linguine with roasted garlic purée, shallots, bell peppers, and white pesto" *or* "warm frisée salad with duck confit, ginger figs, candied walnuts, and grapefruit-tarragon vinaigrette." I said the only thing possible under the circumstances: "Y'all got a combo plate?"

O.K., O.K., so real people live here and have to get root canals; is that any excuse for florists calling themselves "botanical sculptors"? Is the apartment complex I've been living in pink, or is it "shrimp and salmon"? For that matter, are "aubergine, bone, and bisque" foodstuffs or colors?

Assume, just for the sake of argument, that Berkeley is in fact what the rest of the country would be like if it were run by liberals. How does it differ?

Pedestrians have the right of way over cars. Handicapped people not only have the right of way—they're into gonzo-wheelchair competition. Traffic signals to help the blind cross the street don't go beep-beep-beep, as in other places; here they make beautiful bird songs. Dogs have their own parks. Martin Luther King Jr. Boulevard does not run through the black part of town; it runs through a white part of town. There are more little places to stop and drink coffee on Telegraph Avenue than there are days in the year. Except that no one here drinks coffee; they drink cappuccino, espresso, latte, au lait, mocha, and double decaf dooey-bobs.

Also, there are many flowers—flowers growing, flowers in stores, many kinds of flowers. I wouldn't want to stretch the Camelot metaphor too far, but I swear it has rained only at night here for the last three months.

I have seen exactly three women in Berkeley wearing high-heeled shoes, and two of them wore "sensible heels." If there are hookers in this town, they wear Rockports. I heard two people honk. Bumper stickers here are gentle and loving, like TEACH RESPECT FOR THE EARTH AND ALL LIVING THINGS. A Berkeleyite feeling his testosterone may pack a stern message on his car, such as WANT MY VOTE? CUT PENTAGON BLOAT!

Berkeley is bookstore heaven—wonderful, marvelous, fabulous bookstores. And Berkeley being Berkeley, there is also a citizens' organization to support independent bookstores—this is in case you might forget yourself and wander into B. Dalton in search of something definitive on deconstructionism or semiotics.

Personally, I think living in Berkeley is like dwelling with hobbits. Any day now I expect to catch them hiding their furry little feet inside their Birkenstocks. They are so kind and gentle. They all care. They help the homeless. They are proud of their eccentrics. Two of the most notable people in town are the Naked Man and the Pink Man.

A Berkeley story: Some years ago the Berkeley Police Department decided that the drug problem was out of control and that they needed some drug-sniffing dogs to help with enforcement, so they signed up for some trained German shepherds. But locals felt that this might bring up unpleasant memories for Holocaust survivors, besides having Bull Connor overtones, and so they opted for drug-sniffing beagles instead.

Are there Real World problems in Berkeley? Of course. The cost of housing is horrific, but that's true of California as a whole. The poor students live like sardines. The rich folks live on the hills, of course, and the rest of us are in the Flats, a much more interesting part of town.

Diversity is such a political buzzword these days that you can forget what it actually means until you spend time in Berkeley. A stroll across campus or along a Berkeley street is like some PC lesson in multiethnic, multicultural diversity. Black, brown, Japanese, white, Chinese; ashrams, sari shops, Tina Turner Buddhists chanting *ram-rom-om,* bagel shops run by Pakistanis, croissant shops run by Vietnamese, the Black Muslim Bakery; gay and lesbian knitting classes, Little League teams that look like a junior division of the United Nations, Saint Joseph–the-Worker Elementary School featuring Roman Catholics of every nation, skaters with turquoise hair and rings in their noses; God Hill, where all the theological seminaries are clustered.

The right wing, ever behind the cultural curve, is now accusing the left of fostering "identity politics," which means a pernicious harping on one's ethnic heritage. Berkeley is well beyond identity politics. For one thing, everyone seems to have more than one affiliation. Japanese Hispanics, gay Lubavitchers, Finnish acupuncturists, Irish-African-Americans (that's quite a Saint Paddy's Day party). I am told by administrators at UC-Berkeley that the student body is 60 percent "other." Mostly you have to guess. Samoan? Goan? Aztec? At faculty parties I brag that I have a student from Nebraska whose mother makes casseroles with Cheez Whiz.

And what difference does all this ethnic and cultural diversity make (aside from producing some breathtakingly beautiful humans)? In some ways, not much; the students all gripe when you give them homework assignments, no matter what ethnic category they are in. On the other hand, there is some kind of racial sensitivity that sneaks up on you out here. I have been reading the commentary on the current Clinton-administration scandal involving Asian political contributions with horrified fascination. If you were to substitute *Jew* for every reference to *Chinese,* and *Israel* for *China,* the biggest fight since the Dreyfus affair would have broken out by now.

So now it's home to Texas, for the same reasons I always go back to Texas. It's simpler—the bad guys still wear black hats, and the good guys still wear white hats. And it's funnier there—let's face it, the reason we get to laugh more in Texas is because it's just existentially ridiculous. I've been missin' y'all.

Fort Worth Star-Telegram
March 23, 1997

Do Whut? Ooops!

My favorite running story these days is the Year 2000 Problem. This is the wonderful news that come midnight December 31, 1999, all computers will tick over a notch and announce that it is January 1, 1900.

If you believe the most dire analyses of the consequences of this slight misunderstanding, planes will then fall from the sky, ballistic missiles will run amok, global financial markets will crash, hospital life-support systems will shut down, your microwave won't work, your Pontiac won't start, and in general, a fine time will be had by all.

Not being a computer expert, I can't explain why the computers can't figure out the year 2000, except that it seems to be a giant case of "Ooops!" The computer guys forgot to program it in. And for reasons only the experts understand, it is apparently impossible to invent a program to change it now. The only way to fix it is to open every single calendar chip individually—the computer equivalent of going in there with a screwdriver, which is incredibly expensive.

Estimates range from $300 billion to $600 billion worldwide to fix the problem. Ooops.

I am watching this impending global catastrophe play out on the small stage of the Texas Legislature, and what a merry scene it is. Now, far be it from me to paint with a broad brush; we all know there are many people in West Texas who are cosmopolitan, sophisticated, and advanced out the ass. But let's face it: There are also a bunch of West Texans who haven't approved of any technological change since the pickup truck and air-conditioning.

Obviously, we could include East Texas, North Texas, and South Texas in that sweeping statement if we want to, but there is something particularly delicious in the sound of a West Texas legislator listening to some expert explain why the state has to spend hundreds of millions of dollars to fix this doohickey and reacting with a stupefied "Do *whut?*"

This is heaven for every technophobe in America and around the globe. It's the Luddites' revenge; it's the Grumpy Old Reactionaries' Ball. It's sweet satisfaction for every person who has ever been baffled by a computer. It's one in the eye for everyone who can't tell a bit from a byte. The number of "I told you so's" that are going to be flying around for the next few years is infinite. The number of serious thinkers who will be drawing painfully obvious morals from this tale is mind-boggling.

Personally, I think the whole thing can be neatly summed up by "Do *whut?*"

Right now the state's problem is trying to figure out (A) how serious the problem is; and (B) who should fix it. As we might expect of our fellow citizens, many people have already seized upon this lemon and are making lemonade. Companies that are in the business of fixing your Year 2000 problem for a modest arm and a leg are among the hottest stocks on Wall Street. Without naming names, there is a widespread suspicion that some of these folks may be overcharging.

Envision your basic West Texas legislator confronted with the gladsome tidings that the first thing we have to do is hire some consultant who charges $1,000 a day. Next, watch Representative G. E. "Buddy" West of Odessa dealing with the concept of paying $1 million for a thirty-day study of the problem, resulting in a five-page report. "How can you *spend* one million dollars in thirty days?" inquired Buddy West, in a reasonable tone of voice given the circumstances.

Actually, this is a problem many of us are familiar with: Something goes wrong with a major appliance in your home, and you call the guy who charges you $38.50 to come out and look at it and announce that it will cost you at least $300 to fix it. This is just on a slightly larger scale. O.K., a much larger scale.

One would not wish to use the millennium monster as an excuse to bash the cyberworld. On the other hand, I recently heard a speech by Louis Rossetto, editor of *Wired* magazine, on C-SPAN. Rossetto held forth eloquently on the glories of cyberspace; fair enough, but he also denounced all the schnooks who don't get it.

I like *Wired* magazine. I even like the concept of a parallel universe out there in cyberspace, untroubled by failed government and the failed media. A new forum, a new *civitas,* a world where ideas are money and there are no limits. Wow.

So Rossetto oversells a trifle. It was a little like listening to those visionaries in 1969 explain about peace and love and free drugs and rock 'n' roll. I'm sure it will be a better world, and anyone who doesn't get it probably is a schnook. But first someone is going to have to explain it to Buddy West. Ooops.

Fort Worth Star-Telegram
April 22, 1997

Notes from
the Revolution

The Challenge Now Is
to Avoid Being Splattered

Setting aside that Pat Buchanan is a racist, sexist, xenophobic, homophobic anti-Semite, what wonderful news from New Hampshire! It's the nuts! It's the berries!

Yes, well, that is rather a large mound of manure there connected with his name, much of it justified, I'm afraid. There's even more—he defends old Nazis or something.

But since Buchanan has just sent the entire Republican Establishment and half the Democratic Establishment as well into a wall-eyed, blue-bellied snit, what can we do but rejoice?

The good news is that Pat Buchanan—aside from being a racist, sexist, xenophobic, homophobic anti-Semite—is a fairly likable human being. I mean, you'd much rather have a beer with him than Bob Dole or Phil Gramm.

Ask good liberals like Barbara Carlson of Minnesota or Al Franken of the Comedy Channel—they can't help it, in fact. They'd rather not, but they like him.

Numero Two-o, being of the Irish persuasion, Pat Buchanan joys in a good fight, just loves biff-bam-pow, rejoices in a slug fest, gets off on a mud fight. Good thing, since he's in one now. What'll be really fun is watching his fellow Republicans attack him for being a racist, sexist, xenophobic, homophobic anti-Semite, which is not their native turf, as it were.

Somewhere in the Old Testament, it says, "I would that mine enemy had written a book," and Pat Buchanan has. In it, he notes that his father's heroes were Francisco Franco and Senator Joseph McCarthy, which is enough to frizz my hair right there.

On the other hand, I'd hate to have a lot of the stuff I wrote years ago taken out of context and twisted to represent my thinking. But Buchanan is in for it, so he might as well keep up his left.

As near as we can tell, Buchanan's victory in New Hampshire is a pretty much pure win for economic populism. Neither the Christian Coalition nor the anti-abortion movement count for much there, especially compared to Iowa.

What's even more interesting is that the state is not in an economic recession. That vote is a direct reflection of just how worried people are about their future in this two-tier economy. And there's what Bob Herbert calls "a cosmic disconnect" between what people are actually worrying about and what the Republicans are doing in Washington.

There are two problems with Buchanan as a populist.

One is all the divisive gar*bage* he brings with him. It's exactly what has been used to destroy populist surges in the past—setting whites against blacks, natives against immigrants, men against women, straights against gays, Christians against Jews—divide, divide, divide—and lose. Look, Hispanic farmworkers are not responsible for the S&L mess, blacks on welfare are not moving factories to Taiwan, lowering the tax on capital gains is not part of the "gay agenda," and Jews, having been historically discriminated against, by and large support raising the minimum wage.

The second problem is that Buchanan's economic populism is rudimentary. It's one thing to recognize that the gap between the rich and everybody else is growing like a cancer; it's another thing to come up with useful solutions. It's fine to jump on trade and economic globalization, but that's only part of the problem, and not a very big part at that. Nor is git-tough jingoism the solution. Buchanan still favors trickle-down economics—he wants to cut inheritance taxes, the capital-gains tax, and taxes on the rich; that's piss-poor populism and bad economics to boot.

Fort Worth Star-Telegram
February 22, 1996

Let's Not Beat Up on Phil Gramm

Would a bleeding-heart liberal kick a guy while he's down? Should a girl like me, in whom the milk of human kindness flows copiously for everyone from protein-shy Hottentots to the glandular obese, actually aim a few swift boots at the prone form of Senator Phil Gramm? Nah. But it's tempting.

We liberals do sometimes forsake our vows of compassion for all mankind. I recall publicly gloating about the defeat of some of the noxious fatheads Texas used to send to Congress. But hey, I even felt sorry for Richard Nixon when he left; there's nothing you can do about being born liberal—fish gotta swim and hearts gotta bleed.

From the Texas Democratic point of view, it's a shame that Gramm didn't stay in at least through New Hampshire and spend himself broke. Now he'll just come home and clobber some Democrat with his leftover millions. It's hard to write about Gramm without sounding mean; the national reporters' favorite line was, "Even his friends don't like him." The most touching story I ever heard about Gramm was from a fellow senator who used to tell Gramm: "You'll never be president, Phil, because you've got no heart." Gramm, who has more than amply demonstrated his indifference to what his colleagues think of him, for some reason took this guy seriously. For years afterward, whenever he'd done anything that remotely smacked of compassion, he'd come up to this senator and say: "Whatta ya think, whatta ya think—am I showing heart yet?"

Well, it is sort of touching.

What can we say? We elect the guy by two-digit percentage margins, and in the rest of the country he can't buy his way out of single digits with $20 million. And that's just Republicans.

He may be a schmuck, but at least he's our schmuck? (I always think of him as a schmuck from Georgia, but then, I don't like him.) I suppose we could just blame him on the Aggies, but I think that's some kind of -ism—universityism? While Austin snores along in its false sense of superiority, Texas A & M has in fact become a great university. I'm not suggesting that we ban Aggie jokes as politically incorrect, but let's at least recognize reality.

My real problem with Gramm is ill-timed; it's the wrong season to make this case, but I'll try anyway. Set aside that I don't agree with him about anything. I don't agree with Representative Charlie Stenholm, a Blue Dog Democrat, about anything either. But you notice that Stenholm and the rest of the Blue Dogs have been sweating like farmworkers to find a compromise on the budget impasse in Washington. They understand that compromise is necessary.

In this, the era of ideologues, that is a most unfashionable position. There are seventy-three Republican freshmen and one speaker in the House who consider compromise treachery. And Gramm considered compromise treachery before compromise-as-treachery was cool. I suppose we should give him credit for being ahead of his time; Texans always have liked a hard-ass.

Now that *politician* is a dirty word (not that it was ever reminiscent of roses) it seems awfully dated to bring up names like Sam Rayburn, Ralph Yarborough, or Barbara Jordan. But they were politicians. They fought hard, and they compromised, because they thought it was for something quaintly called the greater good. Or maybe they just wanted to move the ball. In any case, in the phrase of the kindergarten report card, they worked and played well with others. And no one ever considered them sissies because of it.

Gramm does not work or play well with others. Never has. And I don't think that works well for Texas. "Get along, go along" is not an inspirational philosophy, and only God knows how much moral cowardice it has covered up over the years. Serve your time, collect your chits, and cash 'em in for your home state? No, I'd say we could ask for more than that from our senators. But I've never seen Phil Gramm collect or cash a chit for anyone except Phil Gramm. And that is one in the ribs to a man who's down.

Fort Worth Star-Telegram
February 15, 1996

Training Dole to Smile

Don't start mourning yet, the fun's not over. True, it has been a festive season for Democrats as the Republicans adopted the D's' popular old circular firing-squad formation.

What glorious material: Steve Forbes, who was manufactured by the same people who make Chatty Cathy dolls, has a battery panel in his back.

I could never get anyone interested in that nice Morry Taylor, the tire guy. Taylor used to answer questions during debates by saying, "Yes." Or, "No." For that alone, he should have been elected president. Just think, a man of few words!

Decent Dick Lugar didn't get any traction: personally, I think his resemblance to Howdy Doody did him in.

Alan Keyes added a touch of the surreal.

Lamar Alexander proved that Dead Men Do Wear Plaid.

But my boy Buchanan soldiers bravely on toward San Diego: whee! Looks as though H. Ross Perot will jump in again—he's good at that. Maybe Buchanan will bolt the party and marry Perot.

Ralph Nader could be on the ballot in twelve states. Here's to another minority president.

And consider Bob Dole, Uriah Heep as undertaker. We now get to watch some of the finest minds of our time, not to mention some of the most expensive, try to convince us that Bob Dole is warm and fuzzy. The man whose response to the State of the Union address brought to mind the words, "Somewhere in Transylvania, there is an empty grave. . . ." Cute, cuddly-like-a-teddy-bear Dole. You notice they've already trained him to smile more, poor man. It's so awful.

Meanwhile, Newt and the Newtzis continue on their merry way. Just what the country needs—more assault weapons. Brought to you by Newt Gingrich, last year's political genius.

You may have noticed a certain dearth of concern for those of the feminine persuasion this year. In fact, so far, we've only come up twice, both times in the South Carolina primary debate. We learned that if either Dole or Buchanan is elected, women who are raped ("by a horrible criminal," specified the questioner) will be forced by law to bear the offspring of same. Dole later recanted this stand and took refuge in perfect obfuscation.

Then all the candidates took turns dumping on Shannon Faulkner, who, having survived one week at the Citadel, now has more military experience than three of the four candidates in that debate.

Not the Year of the Woman so far.

The Progressive
May 1996

Who's Paying for Those Political Campaigns? You'd Be Surprised

Current campaign finance laws restrict corporate political-action committees from giving more than $5,000 to a presidential candidate and limit individuals from giving more than $1,000 to a candidate. According to *The New York Times,* Bob Dole and President Clinton will receive $74 million each for the general election campaign and $12 million each for the convention, all from the pool of funds that we taxpayers provided via our IRS forms to keep the presidential elections honest.

In the meantime, both parties expect to raise another $300 million before the election from corporations and rich individuals, all of it flowing softly and smoothly in unlimited amounts directly to the political parties themselves. In theory, "soft money" is not to go into presidential campaigns but is rather to be spent on voter registration, get-out-the-vote campaigns, and television advertising that does not directly promote a presidential candidate. Shur.

From January to June of this year, both parties had already exceeded all previous soft-money records, with the real campaign yet to come. Naturally both parties officially deplore this highly unfortunate situation, but as they say in many other words, "the other guy is doing it, too"—which is what we used to say during the nuclear arms race.

You may recall that in June of last year, Clinton and House Speaker Newt Gingrich shook hands on an agreement to create a bipartisan commission to reform campaign financing. Nothing ever came of it. A genuinely bipartisan effort at campaign-finance reform (Republican freshman Representative Linda Smith of Washington fought like a Trojan) was killed in Congress.

The corporate special interests are all over the loopholes like a duck on a June bug. Tax-deductible corporate donations to both conventions provided about $25 million per party, in addition to the $12 million in taxpayers' donations. *The New York Times* reports a dandy wrinkle stemming from a Supreme Court decision two months ago: Big donors can give to "independent committees" as long as their activities are not coordinated with those of presidential campaigns. You may recall that it was an "independent committee" that produced the Willie Horton ad against Michael Dukakis in 1988, completely independently of the Bush campaign, of course.

And what do the special interests get in return for these enormous donations? The Center for Responsive Politics offers us a few instructive hints.

One of the matters that Congress is due to resolve before this session is over involves a House provision that prohibits defense contractors from billing the government for costs associated with mergers. Lockheed and Martin Marietta, which merged last year, have already submitted $855 million in bills for their corporate matrimony. Lockheed Martin's PAC's have already contributed $692,350 to federal campaigns this cycle, 73 percent of it to Republicans. All told, defense contractors have given $5.3 million through PAC's, 70 percent to Republicans—all this according to the Project for Government Oversight.

The Small Business Job Protection Act signed by Clinton is pocked with special tax breaks for any number of not-so-small businesses. According to the center, it is worth millions of dollars to auto manufacturers and dealers, the securities and investment industry, and Archer Daniels Midland.

For those who would like to find out precisely how they are being ripped off by this insane system of campaign financing, there is a dandy new Web page called "Follow the Money" run by the Center for Responsive Politics at http://www.crp.org. It enables you to follow political money state by state, and even candidate by candidate and industry by industry. "Follow the Money" also fills you in on the various kinds of reform debates and principles and tells you how you can get involved in the fight to change this massive corruption.

Make no mistake: The special interests that give so generously to political campaigns are not making a foolish investment. They are rewarded with hundreds of millions in special tax breaks and competitive advantages. And you know who winds up paying the tab for that. Whenever a company buys a sweet deal through campaign contributions, the rest of us get stuck with that much more of the tab for keeping the country running and paying for necessary government programs.

You may never have given a nickel to a political campaign in your life, but believe me, they are costing you a fortune.

Fort Worth Star-Telegram
September 12, 1996

Could We Wind Up This Campaign with Some Dignity?

Still hoping that something useful will come out of this dreadful campaign, let's focus again on the money. As the Clinton/Indonesian money connection continues to develop nicely, like a photograph coming up in a chemical bath, we will want to remember a couple of important points.

One is that the problem is not foreign money. I have a vision of us in one of our xenophobic snits deciding that shifty Asians of nefarious intent are out to subvert the Amurkin Way. Follow the money; shifty Asians aren't even in it. Millions and millions in unchecked corporate money is pouring into the parties. No sloe-eyed foreigners—just good ol' red-blooded Amurkin corporations looking for special favors.

According to the Center for Responsive Politics, 52 percent of Americans want major changes in the way campaigns are financed, and another 20 percent believe that we need to make minor changes. And there is a direct correlation between those who know the political system best and those who want to see serious changes. If all we get out of the current mess is a law that says, "No foreign money allowed," we will have blown our best shot for reclaiming a truly representative democracy. We will continue to be governed by a corporate oligarchy.

The good news is that it ain't that hard to fix. Public campaign financing, funded through a voluntary checkoff on the IRS form with a $100 limit, would create a more-than-adequate pool of public financing. Minor parties could qualify for a cut of the money as Ross Perot did, by a decent showing at the polls. Costs can be held down by making free television time available. None of this is new, unheard of, risky, or untried. It's old hat in most European countries.

As for the rest of the sad campaign, Bob Dole could perform one last service for his country by following the Mike Dukakis model. When Dukakis realized that he was going to lose, he did not go quietly, but he did go with dignity. He stopped attacking his opponent and returned to the themes that give Democrats their identity. He preached them with passion (well, with what passes for passion with Dukakis) to ever-larger crowds as the campaign ended.

As a political performance, it was considerably superior to "Where is the outrage in America? Where is the outrage in America? Where has the media gone in America? Where is the outrage in America?"

The other day in University Park, Texas, Dole made the unlikely assertion that "the outrage starts right here at SMU." Right—Southern Methodist University, natural home of outrage. The sorority girls will just whip those bows out of their hair and start a revolution.

Then there was the old media bias theme. "We've got to stop the liberal bias in this country. Don't read that stuff. Don't watch television. You make up your mind. Don't let them make up your mind for you." Dole owes his "outrage" theme to the media, which went out and dug up the Indonesian connection just like we're supposed to, so this seems churlish of him.

As always happens when candidates attack one another instead of promoting their own ideas, we're all left with the impression that we have two terrible people vying for office, that no one has any ideas and the system is so bad that it's not even worth voting.

I'm still unable to discern why Bob Dole thinks his character, whatever that means anymore, is superior to President Clinton's. Better war record, better war—that's about it. Dole has flip-flopped on issues and changed his stands at least as often as Clinton and, given how much longer he's been doing it, probably a lot more often.

I was startled to see that according to two different estimates by two nonpartisan groups, Clinton has kept or tried to keep either 60 or 70 percent of the promises he made during his '92 campaign. The reason that startled me is because I've been buying into all the endless chatter about how he doesn't keep his word, doesn't stand for anything.

An indignant colleague from D.C. in "the liberal media" showed his bias by demanding, "Well, at least you've got to admit Clinton will do anything to get reelected." Look at a rather large "anything" that's been staring the Washington press corps in the face for four years.

What branch of the media can you name that wouldn't kill for an interview with Chelsea Clinton? The duckling with braces on her teeth has turned into a lovely young swan before our eyes; she could be on the cover of every teen mag in the country. Name a newspaper that wouldn't love to interview her, or a television network, or a chat show (Oprah Winfrey, Rosie O'Donnell, Diane Sawyer)—every one of them displaying the charming, poised First Daughter talking about what a wonderful dad our prez is.

Bill Clinton has never exploited his daughter for political purposes. She has gone through what is probably the single worst time of any human's life, her adolescence, without so much as a peep out of the scuzziest tabloids about "Chelsea's First Kiss" or any other nonsense. It takes some seriously hard work to keep a kid in the White House that protected. But her parents are widely deemed not to have a scruple between them.

Meanwhile, Dole is dragging this poor forty-three-year-old woman, his daughter Robin, all over the country with him. As far as anyone knows, they haven't been close since he walked out on her mother when she was eighteen. Character, anyone?

Fort Worth Star-Telegram
October 29, 1996

This Was the Campaign That Was

Those who are profoundly grateful for this presidential election would like to thank all concerned: from Steve Forbes to Bob Dole, from Dick Morris to President Clinton, from the Riady family of Indonesia to Archer Daniels Midland, thank you, one and all. It has been a fabulous year. I believe I speak for the entire community of those who make a living by laughing at politics when I say that we are humbled by the material you have given us.

Let us start back in those glorious days of yesteryear: 1995, when Clinton was dead meat and House Speaker Newt Gingrich bestrode the political world like a Tyrannosaurus rex; when the only question was which Republican would get the nomination and evict Clinton from the White House in a walk.

The first indication we had that it would be an unusually festive year was when class warfare broke out in the Republican party. Senator Phil Gramm announced to an astonished world that he is a "blue-collar Republican." Longtime observers of PACman Phil had to rush home and put cold compresses on their heads. Then My Boy Buchanan started tearing up the pea patch, leading the peasants with pitchforks in a people's insurrection, ranting against the rich, carrying on about corporate greed. He won New Hampshire, and the entire Republican party put a cold compress to its collective head.

Then for a spell President Steve Forbes wandered around the country doing his impersonation of a Chatty Cathy doll. Lamar Alexander was the favored candidate of the charismatically challenged.

The Elephant labored and labored and at last brought forth . . . Bob Dole, an ancient grump but a good fighter. Political conventions entered a new era: tearjerker television, the four-hankie convention. The Democrats had more inspiring handicapped people, but the Republicans topped them with a rape victim. Vice President Al Gore did the macarena.

Meanwhile, Clinton was slowly picking up steam by running on Family Values, a theme introduced to a grateful nation by Dick Morris, the man who liked to play doggie with his prostitute. *Woof, woof!* We couldn't get Colin Powell into the game or Ross Perot out of it. Mark Russell observes that Perot's support is stuck in the single digits, often the middle one.

Dole contributed perhaps the funniest line of the year with his immortal observation that tobacco is not addictive but that too much milk might be bad for us. The check from the dairy lobby must have been late that week.

Then both candidates followed the risky strategy of blowing a hole in the debates by boring the public comatose. Clinton was so on-message that the whole country could do the litany, "Medicare, Medicaid, education, and the environment." The vice-presidential debate set a new high for legal soporifics and raised some serious questions about the War on Drugs. If Jack Kemp had been on downers and Gore had been on speed, it would've been a great debate. Legalize drugs!

Next came a painful period, with Clinton Rose Gardening away while poor Dole sallied forth in pursuit of the Theme of the Week. Theme after theme did nothing for his poll numbers. Finally there was a great public huddle in the Dole camp: Should he play the character card or not? Gosh, the suspense was awful. In the end, to the astonishment of all, he played it, and played it, and played it. (That was the week he took to repeating everything three times.) Liberal, liberal, liberal. Wake up, America. Where is the outrage?

Meanwhile, Clinton had gone a Bridge Too Far in reaching out to the Asian-American community and gotten himself into another pickle over some smelly fund-raising. What's a Clinton campaign without pickles? Smelly fund-raising was a bipartisan sport this year; we had a wide range of smells, but they were all awful. While Dole was bashing the liberal media, the liberal media were chasing Clinton's Indonesian connection and ignoring the record criminal fine levied against the vice chairman of Dole's finance committee. The daring and the foolish actually believe that Some Good Will Come from all this; cross your fingers, patriots, and think Campaign-Finance Reform.

Now the days dwindle down to a precious (?) few, and the only question left is whether we're going to vote Newt back into power. The trouble with reelecting Newt is that we'll have to listen to him for another two years. Newt suffers from what the shrinks call projection—he's always accusing other people of what he does himself. Which leads me to believe he is best described by his own favorite adjectives, the ones he uses so constantly that they are as familiar as that bridge to the twenty-first century: "bizarre, sick, pathetic, twisted, and grotesque."

As for the presidential race, Mark Russell leaves us with this happy thought: Cheer up—one of them will lose.

Fort Worth Star-Telegram
October 31, 1996

Lyin' Bully

One of the things that concerns a lot of Americans lately is the increase in plain old nastiness in our political discussion. It comes from a number of sources, but Rush Limbaugh is a major carrier.

I should explain that I am not without bias in this matter. I have been attacked by Rush Limbaugh on the air, an experience somewhat akin to being gummed by a newt. It doesn't actually hurt, but it leaves you with slimy stuff on your ankle.

I have a correspondent named Irwin Wingo in Weatherford, Texas. Irwin and some of the leading men of the town are in the habit of meeting about ten every morning at the Chat & Chew Café to drink coffee and discuss the state of the world. One of their number is a dittohead, a Limbaugh listener. He came in one day, plopped himself down, and said, "I think Rush is right: Racism in this country is dead. I don't know what the niggers will find to gripe about now."

I wouldn't say that dittoheads, as a group, lack the ability to reason. It's just that whenever I run across one, he seems to be at a low ebb in reasoning skills. Poor ol' Bill Sarpalius, one of our dimmer Panhandle congressmen, was once trying to explain to a town-hall meeting of his constituents that Limbaugh was wrong when he convinced his listeners that Bill Clinton's tax package contained a tax increase on the middle class. (It increased taxes only on the wealthiest 2 percent of Americans.) Sarp claimed he had considered all the facts and cast a vote based on his intelligence and judgment. A dittohead in the crowd rose to protest: "We don't send you to Washington to make intelligent decisions. We send you there to represent us."

The kind of humor Limbaugh uses troubles me deeply, because I have spent much of my professional life making fun of politicians. I believe it is a great American tradition and should be encouraged. We should all laugh more at our elected officials—it's good for us and good for them. So what right do I have to object because Limbaugh makes fun of different people than I do?

I object because he consistently targets dead people, little girls, and the homeless—none of whom are in a particularly good position to answer back. Satire is a weapon, and it can be quite cruel. It has historically been the weapon of powerless people aimed at the powerful. When you use satire against powerless people, as Limbaugh does, it is not only cruel, it's profoundly vulgar. It is like kicking a cripple.

On his TV show, early in the Clinton administration, Limbaugh put up a picture of Socks, the White House cat, and asked, "Did you know there's a White House dog?" Then he put up a picture of Chelsea Clinton, who was thirteen years old at the time and as far as we know had never done any harm to anyone.

When viewers objected, he claimed, in typical Limbaugh fashion, that the gag was an accident and that without his permission some technician had put up the picture of Chelsea—which I found as disgusting as his original attempt at humor.

On another occasion, Limbaugh put up a picture of Labor Secretary Robert Reich that showed him from the forehead up, as though that were all the camera could get. Reich is indeed a very short man as a result of a bone disease he had as a child. Somehow the effect of bone disease in children has never struck me as an appropriate topic for humor.

The reason I take Rush Limbaugh seriously is not because he's of-

fensive or right-wing, but because he is one of the few people addressing a large group of disaffected people in this country. And despite his
frequent denials, Limbaugh does indeed have a somewhat cultlike effect on his dittoheads. They can listen to him for three and a half hours
a day, five days a week, on radio and television. I can assure you that
David Koresh did not harangue the Branch Davidians so long nor so
often. But that is precisely what most cult leaders do—talk to their
followers hour after hour after hour.

A large segment of Limbaugh's audience consists of white males,
eighteen to thirty-four years old, without college education. Basically,
a guy I know and grew up with named Bubba.

Bubba listens to Limbaugh because Limbaugh gives him someone
to blame for the fact that Bubba is getting screwed. He's working
harder, getting paid less in constant dollars, and falling further and
further behind. Not only is Bubba never gonna be able to buy a house,
he can barely afford a trailer. Hell, he can barely afford the payments
on the pickup.

And because Bubba understands he's being shafted, even if he
doesn't know why or how or by whom, he listens to Limbaugh. Limbaugh offers him scapegoats. It's the "feminazis." It's the minorities.
It's the limousine liberals. It's all these people with all these wacky social programs to help some silly, self-proclaimed bunch of victims.
Bubba feels like a victim himself—and he is—but he never got any
sympathy from liberals.

Often psychologists tell us there is a great deal of displaced anger
in our emotional lives—your dad wallops you, but he's too big to hit
back, so you go clobber your little brother. Displaced anger is also
common in our political life. We see it in this generation of young
white men without much education and very little future. This economy no longer has a place for them. The corporations have moved
their jobs to Singapore. Unfortunately, it is Limbaugh and the Republicans who are addressing the resentments of these folks and aim-
ing their anger in the wrong direction.

In my state, I have not seen so much hatred in politics since the heyday of the John Birch Society in the early 1960s. In those days you couldn't talk politics with a conservative without his getting all red in the face, arteries standing out in his neck, wattles aquiver with indignation—just like a turkey gobbler. And now we're seeing the same kind of anger again.

★

Fairness & Accuracy in Reporting, the organization that provided the absurd Limbaughisms collected below, has a sweet, gentle faith that truth will triumph in the end and thinks it is sufficient to point out that Limbaugh is wrong. I say it's important to point out that he's not just wrong but that he's ridiculous, one of the silliest people in America. Sure, it takes your breath away when he spreads some false and vicious rumor, such as the story that Vincent Foster's body was actually discovered in a love nest he shared with Hillary Clinton. Or when he destroys an important lobby-control bill by falsely claiming that it would make the average citizen subject to lobbying laws. Yes, that's sick and perverse.

But it's important to show people that there is much more wrong with Limbaugh's thinking than just his facts. Limbaugh specializes in ad hominem arguments, which are themselves ridiculously easy to expose. Ted Kennedy says, "America needs health-care reform." Limbaugh replies, "Ted Kennedy is fat."

Rush Limbaugh's pathetic abuse of logic, his absurd pomposity, his relentless self-promotion, his ridiculous ego—now those, friends, are appropriate targets for satire.

A Spin Doctorate in Reaganomics

Limbaugh: "Don't let the liberals deceive you into believing that a decade of sustained growth without inflation in America (in the '80s) resulted in a bigger gap between the have and the have-nots. Figures compiled by the Congressional Budget Office dispel that myth" (Limbaugh, *The Way Things Ought to Be,* p. 70).

Reality: CBO numbers for after-tax incomes show that in 1980 the richest fifth of our country had eight times the income of the poorest fifth. By 1989, the ratio was more than 20-to-1.

More Bogus Economics

Limbaugh: "The poorest people in America are better off than the mainstream families of Europe" (radio, 1993).

Reality: The poorest 20 percent of Americans can purchase an average of $5,433 worth of goods with their income. Meanwhile, in Germany, the average person can purchase $20,610 worth of goods; in France, $19,200; in Britain, $16,730 (*World Development Report 1994,* published by the World Bank).

Making Ends Meet

Limbaugh: On the official poverty line: "$14,400 for a family of four. That's not so bad" (radio, Nov. 9, 1993).

Versus Limbaugh: A few months earlier, Limbaugh was talking about how tough it was to live on more than 10 times that: "I know families that make $180,000 a year and they don't consider themselves rich. Why, it costs them $20,000 a year to send their kids to school" (radio, Aug. 3, 1993).

A Poor Excuse

Limbaugh: "All of these rich guys—like the Kennedy family and Perot—pretending to live just like we do and pretending to understand our trials and tribulations and pretending to represent us, and they get away with this" (TV, Nov. 18, 1993).

Versus Limbaugh: Limbaugh's income was an estimated $25 million over the last two years (*Forbes,* Sept. 26, 1994).

The Mis-State of Black America

Limbaugh: "So many people are either refusing to recognize or unable to recognize the difference between blacks who riot and the majority of blacks in the American middle class. According to University of Chicago sociologist William Julius Wilson, of the 29 million blacks in America, the largest percentage—35 percent— are upper middle class, both professional (lawyer, doctor) and white collar; 32 percent are middle class; and 33 percent are considered poor" (*Ought to Be,* p. 224).

Reality: Wilson actually says that 20 percent of blacks are in the "professional middle class," which includes teachers and nurses, and that a further 15 percent are in "nonprofessional white-collar positions," such as secretarial or sales jobs. Limbaugh deceptively calls all these "upper middle class"—a description that hardly fits teachers, let alone salesclerks. The category Limbaugh calls "middle class" Wilson refers to as "working class," who he says are "vulnerable to job loss through economic restructuring" (*Los Angeles Times,* May 6, 1992).

Missing the Forest for . . . Missing the Forest

Limbaugh: "There are more acres of forestland in America today than when Columbus discovered the continent in 1492" (Limbaugh, *See, I Told You So,* p. 171).

Reality: Forestland in what are now the 50 states covered about 1 billion acres before European settlement, according to U.S. Forest Service historian Douglas MacCleery. Today, there are only 737 million acres of forestland, much of which lacks the ecological diversity of old-growth forest (the American Forestry Association).

Following the Lead Rodent

Limbaugh: Frequently denies that he uses his show for political activism: "I have yet to encourage you people or urge you to call anybody. I don't do it. They think I'm the one doing it. That's fine. You don't need to be told when to call. They think you are a bunch of lemmings out there" (radio, June 28, 1993).

Reality: One hour later, he urged his followers into action against Clinton's tax package: "The people in the states where these Democratic senators are up for re-election in '94 have to let their feelings be known. . . . Let's say Herb Kohl is up in '94. You people in Wisconsin who don't like this bill, who don't like the tax increases, you let Herb Kohl know somehow."

True Rush

On "The Homeless Trap," a work of art that employs a large mouse-traplike device and uses a bedroll as bait: "I've got this idea. Instead of one of these, have 1,000 of them. And use them as a solution—not as a piece of art. Just put these things all over the city and if they trap homeless people, use them" (TV, March 9, 1994).

"This is asinine! A Cesar Chavez Day in California? Wasn't he convicted of a crime?" (radio, 1994).

"I don't give a hoot that [Columbus] gave some Indians a disease that they didn't have immunity against" (*Ought to Be,* p. 45).

On the endangered northern spotted owl: "If the owl can't adapt to the superiority of humans, screw it" (*Ought to Be,* p. 162).

"The NAACP should have riot rehearsal. They should get a liquor store and practice robberies" (radio; reported in the *Flush Rush Quarterly,* January 1993).

On Tipper Gore's decision to give up her career for the sake of her marriage: "If you want a successful marriage, let your husband do what he wants to do. . . . You women don't realize how fortunate you are to be watching this show. I have just spelled out for you the key ingredient to a successful marriage" (TV, Feb. 23, 1994).

"I think this reason why girls don't do well on multiple choice tests goes all the way back to the Bible, all the way back to Genesis, Adam and Eve. God said, 'All right, Eve, multiple choice or multiple orgasms, what's it going to be?' We all know what was chosen" (TV, Feb. 23, 1994).

Mother Jones
May/June 1995

Stand By, America!
Newt Alert!

The most fun guy to watch in the New Regime is House Speaker–elect Newt Gingrich. The reason you want to keep an eye on Gingrich is that he plans to improve your morality, and he's just the fellow to do it.

You may not have had the improvement of your morality in mind when you voted to get the government off your back Tuesday, but here in the New Regime, many things are wondrous.

Gingrich explained to *The New York Times* the other day that the country has been in a state of moral decline since the 1960s and that he plans to root out the remnants of the counterculture and the Great Society. Said Gingrich: "Until the mid-1960s, there was an explicit, long-term commitment to creating character. It was the work ethic. It was honesty, right and wrong. It was not harming others. It was being vigilant in the defense of liberty."

Yep, you want to know right from wrong, you check with Newt here in the New Regime, because Newt knows.

Gingrich spent the early part of the dread 1960s at Emory University in Atlanta, at a time when many who felt strongly about morality were involved in the civil-rights movement. He was not. Like President Clinton, being a graduate student—in Gingrich's case, already married with children—kept him out of Vietnam; then he went to Tulane, where he was also not involved in the preeminent moral issue of the late 1960s. Like Clinton, the only nonpolitical job he has ever held was teaching college: Clinton taught constitutional law at the University of Arkansas; Gingrich taught history at West Georgia College.

Gingrich, the man who put term limits in the Contract with America, was first elected to Congress in 1978, after two earlier, unsuccessful races. He was, of course, strong on family values. In 1981 he filed for a divorce from his longtime wife, Jacqueline. According to media reports, during their separation Gingrich went to see Jacqueline in the hospital, where she was recovering from cancer surgery, to discuss the terms of their divorce. Years later, in 1993, Jacqueline would sue Newt for not paying his $1,300-a-month alimony on time.

In the famous flap about the House bank, Gingrich was found to have bounced twenty-two checks, compared with Speaker Tom Foley's two.

But easily the most notable contribution to our political life made by Gingrich during his congressional career has been the level of rancor and vitriol with which he practices politics. So impressive were Gingrich's thrusts at the opposition that in 1990, the GOP issued a list of them—words that Republican candidates should use to describe their opponents so they could be successful, like Newt. The words are *sick, pathetic, traitor, welfare, crisis, ideological, cheat, steal, insecure, bizarre, permissive, anti-(issue),* and *radical.*

Let's look at that list again, because we're going to be hearing quite a lot from Mr. Gingrich, and not only in person. As he has announced, he will be using Rush Limbaugh and Christian-right radio and television programs to communicate his ideas. *Sick, pathetic, traitor, welfare, crisis, ideological, cheat, steal, insecure, bizarre, permissive, anti-(issue),* and *radical.*

Such language, here in the New Regime, will be helpful in solving problems, such as how to get health-care coverage for forty million Americans, how to get people off welfare, how to create decent-paying jobs and give people the skills to do them.

Mickey Kaus of *The New Republic* gives us a typical example of how Gingrich does politics. You may recall the flapette late in the mercifully over elections concerning a memo written by Alice Rivlin, one of the most consistently realistic deficit hawks in the Clinton administration. Rivlin outlined a number of options for further cutting the deficit and still finding ways to invest in programs, particularly job-skills programs. Among her options was cutting Social Security benefits to the wealthy. This was seized upon by Gingrich, who promptly raised an enormous furor about how Clinton was planning to cut Social Security. Clinton brilliantly riposted that he wasn't planning to cut it but that the Republicans were. Are not, are so, are not, they argued, which was the level of debate we got throughout the elections.

Kaus went and found Gingrich's 1986 Social Security proposal that advocates cutting off Social Security for everyone in the country under forty and then passing a national value-added tax (VAT) of $200 billion per year. But—this is the beauty part—Gingrich had accused Rivlin and Clinton of hypocrisy. Which brings us to the First Rule of Newt-Watching: Whatever he accuses his opponents of, look for carefully in his own behavior.

Gingrich recently told a group of lobbyists he was, to put it crudely, shaking down, that his election strategy was to portray Clinton Democrats as "the enemy of normal Americans" and proponents of "Stalinist measures." I'm fond of hyperbole myself. But when politicians start talking about large groups of their fellow Americans as "enemies," it's time for a quiet stir of alertness. Polarizing people is a good way to win an election, and also a good way to wreck a country. Stay alert.

Fort Worth Star-Telegram
November 13, 1994

The Pod People
Take Over Congress

WASHINGTON, D.C. — I always did think the Washington press corps had played center too long (old joke: The center sees the world backward and upside down), and now I know it. For three months, we have been reading about "the new leadership" in Washington. People have devoted long and solemn thumb-suckers to the new leadership, analyzed it, psychoanalyzed it, and worked it by fractions. Ignoring, of course, the real story, which is not the new leadership here but the new followership.

The government has been taken over by YAFers. All you onetime college students will remember YAFers—the Young Americans for Freedom—who used to bustle around campus in those dorky suits, like Mormons on speed. Well, now they're in Congress. Some of the new representatives were just Young Republicans in college, rather than YAFers, which is worse news, because at least YAF had that nice, goofy subset of libertarians who were a lot of fun. Young Republicans were never fun.

Boy, are these people followers. Lock step, in line, march in unison, chant in unison, don't think, don't learn, follow the leader. I'm telling you, Representative Sonny Bono is one of the intellectual giants among the Republican freshmen. In addition to this awful sort of frat-boy rah-rah attitude, the new Repubs haven't even the grace to be humble, which is the proper role of any freshperson. A very distinguished and couth man said—under one of those Washington journalism rules where you're not allowed to name any of the people you quote—"I just want to *slap* them."

Here's an example of why one might want to slap a Republican congressional follower. You may recall a particularly puzzling bit of mean-spiritedness in the Republican recision bill: the decision to cut the Supplemental Security Income that goes to poor children with crippling conditions such as spina bifida. Their specific problem with this otherwise logical program (the supplemental income enables families to care for their own kids instead of having the government pay to send them to a hellaciously expensive institution—not even pro-family) was that the number of people receiving SSI has gone up considerably in the past few years. Soared, you might say.

So, the Republicans announced, poor people were clearly coaching their children to *fake* crippling conditions. The mind-boggling notion of a four-year-old faking spina bifida did not give the Republican followers so much as a single pause. They gravely recited this rationale, apparently believed it with the greatest of ease, and cut the program.

Then the leadership role appeared. The followers charge, and House Speaker Newt Gingrich, needing to get out in front of his own troops, then carries their weird notions to new heights of bizarreness. Gingrich told the U.S. Chamber of Commerce, in a speech reported by Lars-Erik Nelson of *Newsday,* that poor people were not only coaching their kids on how to fake disability but *beating them if they do not succeed.* "They're being punished for not getting what they call crazy money, or stupid money. We are literally having children suffering child abuse so they can get a check for their parents." So, Gingrich concluded, this program encourages child abuse.

Now we're not just talking fraud and fakery but horrible brutality.

Why did the SSI rolls go up dramatically, and who helped make it happen? Here's the real story. While the Republicans controlled the White House, programs like SSI were run at the speed of molasses. The result was a great pile-up of applications for SSI. People who applied were first rejected automatically; then they had to file an appeal, then the appeals stacked up, and so on and so forth.

You might think this saved the government money, but no. It turns out that seriously ill people with few resources have to go to the hospital to die, and that costs a lot more money than the home care they can get with SSI, so this cruel delaying tactic actually made the deficit worse. Then some influential people, including Representative Carrie Meek of Florida and others, started pushing the SSI bureaucracy, which then started moving faster on the backed-up applications, and lots more people were enrolled in SSI. Not because poor people beat crippled children, but because some bigwigs goosed the bureaucrats.

The weirdest thing about this exercise in Republican fantasy is that anyone could possibly have believed it in the first place. May I offer a suggestion as to what the problem might be? I think economic segregation in this country is so rigid that we literally don't know one another anymore. Republicans just don't know any people on welfare or SSI; they grow up in the suburbs, go to pretty schools, get a good education, and think everyone in the country should be able to make it "on their own" the way *they* did. As Jim Hightower says, "Born on third and thinks he hit a triple."

Which is why sensible people could entertain such lurid fantasies about "the poor," whom they think of as The Other. It's either that or the entire Republican freshman class is a bunch of nutters.

When I think of the love, care, devotion, and patience I have seen lavished on disabled children by their struggling parents, and then I read Gingrich's cruel, ugly, wicked distortions, I want to slap somebody, too.

Fort Worth Star-Telegram
April 6, 1995

No Shit, Sherlock! Why the Government Shut Down

Whee! Spin City. Who's responsible for shutting down the federal government and quite possibly sending the financial markets into a hopeless tizz?

"You hit me first."

"Did not."

"Did too."

"Did so."

"Did not."

We live in a great nation. Amen.

Actually, taking the popular, fail-safe, appearin'-as-wise-as-a-treeful-of-owls, plague-on-both-their-houses position here is as gutless as it is easy.

The who-to-blame conundrum is just not that tough a nut to crack, although it appears to have sent the Washington press corps back into the most timid form of objectivity: "We only report what other people say; we do not find the facts." For example, here's a dandy story from the Associated Press reporting on how we got into this pickle: "Clinton said Gingrich promised in the spring to force a budget crisis, if necessary, to impose the GOP will." Now, how much effort does it take to determine that House Speaker Newt Gingrich said exactly that, at several times in several places? He did, he did, as we Texans say.

Don't know if you were privileged to hear Gingrich on Saturday blaming the entire impasse on President Clinton, but it was a bravura performance. He sounded exactly like Oliver Hardy saying to Stan Laurel, "Here's another fine mess you've gotten us into." Unable to restrain himself, Gingrich also took several cheap shots at Clinton for having gone off to play golf after announcing that he wouldn't sign a continuing budget resolution draped with extraneous matter, including a Medicare premium increase. The idea of Clinton golfing(!) at such a time almost rendered the speaker apoplectic; the implication was that this president (a word that Gingrich manages to invest with contempt) is a lazy do-nothing.

Now, there are many things for which Clinton can be criticized, but not working hard enough is not one of them. His famous fifteen-hour days are a matter of record and legend. As a matter of negotiating technique, when you have to resolve a critical issue with an unfriendly adversary, it is not wise to start out blaming everything on your opposite number and then taking cheap shots at same. This is ill-advised. Unproductive.

Clinton never gets credit for anything, so let me bravely swim against the entire Washington press corps and point out that the president, faced for the past eleven months with the most hostile, nasty, relentlessly partisan Congress we have ever seen, has behaved like a real grown-up. In fact, I wish Virginia Clinton Kelley were still around so I could congratulate her on having taught that man good manners.

It is true that while out on the campaign trail, at clearly political rallies, Clinton has taken some shots at the Republicans and engaged in a little ridicule of them. But when he is in Washington, speaking as president, he has been consistently mannerly, serious, and (in the opinion of this liberal populist) more than adequately ready to reach compromise. To now blame Clinton for the current budget impasse is outside of enough, and it's high time someone said so.

Lee Howell, former press secretary to Gingrich, said: "There is the Newt Gingrich who is the intellectual, appealing and fun to be with. And there's the Newt Gingrich who is the bloodthirsty partisan who'd just as soon cut your guts out as look at you. And who, very candidly, is mean as hell."

On November 29, 1994, Gingrich himself said, "We don't particularly want to have a single ounce of compromise with those who still believe they can somehow improve and prop up and make work a bureaucratic welfare state."

My own modest contribution to Gingrichiana is the observation that the man regularly accuses others of that of which he is guilty himself. In a recent attack on Clinton, Gingrich said, "When you have a president who is capable of making up whatever fantasies fit his current position, I don't know how as a serious person you can do anything."

I am informed that this is a phenomenon well known to psychiatrists; I've never seen it so clearly or so often in politics before. Pardon me, but I see no reason to pretend to objectivity on this. The facts are there, and the record is there—we can all fairly blame Newt Gingrich for this fine mess.

The Progressive
November 1995

Favorite moment in the Great Budget Impasse (so far):

According to *USA Today,* at Monday's late-night budget meeting, House Majority Leader Dick Armey, Texas's own, took offense when President Clinton pointed his finger at him. That sort of thing isn't done in Texas, Armey said. In Arkansas, Clinton replied icily, politicians don't attack another politician's wife.

It's a little unclear which insult to his wife Clinton had in mind. In

1993 Armey told a convention of real estate agents in Plano that "Hillary Clinton bothers me a lot. I realized the other day her thoughts sound a lot like Marx. She hangs around a lot of Marxists. All her friends are Marxists."

A few months later, Armey described the First Lady's health plan as the "Dr. Kevorkian description for the jobs of American working men and women." Several days later Armey was questioning Hillary during a health-care hearing and said he hoped it would be a lively hearing. She replied, "I'm sure it will, with you and Dr. Kevorkian."

Armey then said, "I have been told about your charm and wit, and let me say reports of your charm are overstated and reports of your wit are understated." (An old line, borrowed for the occasion.)

As a matter of strict accuracy, Armey, who was raised in North Dakota and arrived in Texas at about age thirty, is incorrect. We have a number of Texas politicians who are habitual finger-pointers, Governor George W. Bush and Lieutenant Governor Bob Bullock notable among them.

These Republicans are slow learners. In mid-budget crisis, they keep making things worse. One addition to the budget is a jigger to make the $500-per-child tax credit retroactive to October 1, so folks get a $125 break in an election year. But they made the capital-gains tax cut retroactive to January 1, and most people with capital gains earn more than $100,000 a year.

"The plan sets an early starting date for the tax benefits most affecting upper-income Americans and a later date for the middle-class cuts," reported *USA Today*.

The great mystery remains: If the Republicans think a balanced budget is so all-fired important, how come they've got $245 billion worth of tax cuts in this package, most of it going to rich people?

Let me confess the obvious: Journalists are having a ball with this. There's nothing we like better than crisis. The bustle, the sense of self-importance. Give it a few days, and the Budget Impasse will have its own logo on television news programs, just like the Persian Gulf War. Standoff at Gucci Gulch, perhaps? Showdown at the PU Corral?

Oh, the fake drama of it all. Ah, the delicious posturing, the yummy pretense of unendurable indignation, the fabulous "Who, me?" routines. Eventually, of course, the public will say, "Why don't you dorks get off the dime?" and it will all be resolved in an instant. Until then, we can count on our stalwart public servants to milk this for every second of television time they can.

Fort Worth Star-Telegram
November 14 and 16, 1995

Gingrich: Using Tragedy as Fuel for Scorched-Earth Politics

The first time it happened, I thought it was just another instance of House Speaker Newt Gingrich being despicable. The second time, I figured it proved he was a moron. But now that it has happened a third time, I think we should look at the pattern and its purpose.

In October 1994, when Susan Smith, a desperately disturbed woman, drowned her two small children and tried to blame it on a fictitious black stranger, Gingrich—who is not an expert in crime, psychology, or social pathology but who is a politician without scruples—was ready with an explanation.

"I think the mother killing her two children in South Carolina vividly reminds every American how sick society is getting and how much we have to have change. I think people want to change, and the only way you get change is to vote Republican."

The facts argued rather persuasively against the speaker's thesis. Smith's father had committed suicide when she was six. She tried to commit suicide at the age of thirteen. Mental-health experts said she was dangerously depressed and recommended that she be hospitalized, but her mother refused.

If it can be argued that anyone besides Smith is responsible for the death of her children, it would be her stepfather, Beverly Russell, who began sexually abusing Susan when she was fifteen and continued sleeping with her during and after her marriage until just two months before she committed murder. Neither Smith's mother nor local social workers would help her when she went to them as a teenager and reported Russell's sexual abuse.

Russell was a leader in the Christian Coalition and a member of the state Republican executive committee, yet no sane person would blame either the Christian Coalition or the Republican party for Smith's tragic act—unless, of course, there were a Democratic politician somewhere as unscrupulous as Gingrich.

The second case was the fatal shooting of a three-year-old on a gang-infested street in Los Angeles. Stephanie Kuhen was killed and her family injured in a drive-by shooting. Gingrich's contribution on that sad occasion was to characterize a suspect's being on parole as "a glaring example of a liberal, New Deal approach that put up with violence, accepted brutality."

The connection with the New Deal may not leap to your mind, as neither liberals nor New Dealers have ever been much noted for putting up with violence or brutality. Nonviolence and efforts to stop brutality are rather more the hallmarks of liberals than of conservatives, from the civil-rights movement to Amnesty International. But Gingrich is not one to let an opportunity for demagoguery pass by.

The current case is the hideous slaying of Debra Evans, a mother on welfare who was nine months pregnant, and two of her children. Three people, including a former boyfriend of Evans's, are accused of the crime and of having cut the unborn child from Evans's body. This time Gingrich decided to blame the welfare system, even though it was the victims who were on welfare.

"It happened in America because for two generations we haven't had the guts to talk about right and wrong," said Gingrich, the great moral arbiter. "Let's talk about what the welfare state has created. Let's talk about the moral decay of the world the left is defending."

Evans, the welfare mother, was a regular churchgoer known for opening her home and sharing what little food she had with others; she and her two children were each buried with Bibles on their chests.

Now, in none of these cases does Gingrich's attempt to use tragedy for political purposes make one iota of logical sense. I could just as well argue that Evans is dead because one of her alleged murderers wanted a child and followed the Republican doctrine of greed and selfishness: Me-me-me, get out of my way, I can take what I want, I don't care who it hurts or what it pollutes, I am not my brother's keeper, I don't want laws or regulations standing in my way, greed is good, don't take my tax money to help other people, the strong should take what they want and forget the weak. Look, it's all the Republicans' fault.

Of course, that doesn't make an iota of logical sense either. But Gingrich's pattern does; it's the Big Lie technique. If he keeps associating horrible tragedies with liberalism or welfare, some people are bound to accept the association without thinking about it. This is more than just another case of Gingrich-popping-off-again. Gingrich is not just skipping blithely over logic; he is also abandoning responsibility for any reasonable discussion about what can be done to improve the welfare system or any other part of government.

Gingrich doesn't address issues; he only spouts a particularly brutal form of spin. The man is a political sociopath.

Fort Worth Star-Telegram
November 26, 1995

Fragrant It's Not

Pee-yew! Just trying to get a count on all the sneaky antienvironmental stuff now floating through Congress like fecal coliform bacteria is a major journalistic sewage project. Tucked away in riders here, amendments there, in little zits on the appropriations bill, are so many measures to damage the environment that it amounts to one big stink.

One of the funnier documents in the big stink pile is a Republican-party memo advising members on how to appear concerned about the environment. They recommend that GOPers hold public tree plantings (!)—and invite the press, of course. And that they tour high-tech cleanup companies—and invite the press, of course. That they join the boards of their local zoos and garden clubs; House Speaker Newt Gingrich publicizes his involvement with the Atlanta Zoo.

None of this reverses one iota of the damage being done to the environment by Republican proposals, but hey, in politics, appearance is everything.

Actually, it's not that there are no Republican proposals on the environment; there are only moves to repeal, cutback, downsize, eliminate, or reverse existing environmental protections. No one actually favors dirty air or filthy water, so this is a politically tricky feat.

You first have to demonize those who care about the environment. The above-mentioned memo refers to "attacks by the environmentalist lobby and their extremist friends in the eco-terrorist underworld" and "the green extremists." Always good to identify the opposition with extremism and terrorism.

Meanwhile, the environment, which does not respond to political spin, is out there quietly degrading away. The Environmental Protection Agency had its budget reduced by about one third in September. Even under a temporary funding arrangement, the agency has had to cancel inspections at hundreds of factories and other facilities around the country. Malfunctioning sewage systems, polluted drinking water, fish tainted with mercury—all sorts of dandy stuff is now utterly unchecked.

Meanwhile, the logging companies are getting permission to cut in national forests, including some of the last of the old-growth timber stands. Mining companies are looting merrily; the ranchers have got a proposed moratorium on grazing regulations; the National Biological Service is being eliminated; salmon and trout habitats in the Pacific Northwest are back open for plunder, and so on and so forth. The total list is truly staggering.

One of the major players in all this is Texas Representative Tom DeLay, the former bug exterminator from Fort Bend County, who calls the EPA "a Gestapo organization." DeLay, among his other nuthatch hobby horses, is convinced that there is no problem with the ozone layer and so there is no need to ban chlorofluorocarbons. Unimpressed by the report of the World Meteorological Association or any of the dozens of others, he refers to the committee that gave the Nobel Prize to the two scientists who first identified the ozone problem as "a bunch of Swedish environmental extremists."

DeLay, the Republican majority whip, last year assembled the group known as Project Relief—more than one hundred business lobbies dedicated to stopping federal regulation of business. The 115 political-action committees now associated with Project Relief gave House members more than $10.3 million in campaign contributions in 1993–94, according to an Environmental Working Group study of Federal Election Commission records.

According to *The Washington Post,* the collection of business and industry lobbyists met in DeLay's office, and Gordon Gooch—a lobbyist for the petrochemical industry—wrote the first draft of a bill that would impose a moratorium on all new federal regulation, even for health and safety.

In the old days at the Texas Lege, polluters used to defend themselves with such memorable declarations as "Cyanide is a scare word." Polluters don't seem to have learned much. Among the seventeen pollution riders originally attached to the EPA budget bill were those opposing restricting lead in the air and radon and arsenic (another scare word) in tap water and exempting industrial plants from water-pollution controls.

In terms of wilderness, Utah and Alaska are in the greatest danger—with the happy acquiescence of their Republican representatives. Utah could lose 4.4 million acres of wilderness protection in that glorious red-rock country, which is absolutely unique. But most of the crimes against the environment now sneaking through Congress are not of the backpacker/bird-lover variety: they are basic health and safety measures. You don't have to give a flying fart about the tufted titmouse to find the prospect of arsenic in your tap water unappetizing.

Fort Worth Star-Telegram
December 17, 1995

Funhouse Admittance? Just Your Sanity, Mrs. Clinton

A well-informed woman, interested in politics, inquired a few days ago: "I keep trying to follow this, but I still don't understand: Just what is it Hillary Clinton is accused of?"

Beats me. I keep listening to Senator Alfonse D'Amato, a punishing assignment in itself, and I don't get it either. Of course, having D'Amato conduct an ethics investigation is like watching Mike Tyson run a sensitivity-training seminar. As I understand it, D'Amato—by straining at gnats and putting on a display of prosecutorial innuendo unrivaled since the days of Joe McCarthy—hopes to make the case that the First Lady personally ordered the firings of everyone who worked for the White House travel office when Clinton first came in—which, were it the case, would not be illegal, immoral, or unethical.

He has further sought, with great fervor, to prove that Hillary Clinton did some legal work for James McDougal's long-since-failed S&L, which we know to be true because (A) she told us so years ago; and (B) all the papers turned over to D'Amato's committee bear her out. ?????
That she did so is also not illegal, immoral, or unethical.

For some reason, all of this inspires D'Amato—who always was easy to excite—to wander around talking about "bombshells" and "smoking guns." D'Amato claims that there are "tremendous discrepancies" in what the First Lady has said. She said that the work she did for Madison Guaranty Savings & Loan was "minimal." The billing records show that she did sixty hours of work for the S&L over fifteen months—less than an hour a week. *Quel* tremendous discrepancy.

The funniest day so far in D'Amato's Funhouse was when a fellow whom Hillary Clinton had described as a "young lawyer" who originally brought the McDougal business to her firm came to testify. D'Amato had promised the press, per usual, that his testimony would be "a bombshell." The press duly reported the night before that "a bombshell" was expected at the hearing. The "young lawyer," now bald as a billiard ball and distinctly middle-aged, shows up, reminding all hands that we are now trying to get people to remember, in excruciating detail, what happened fifteen years ago.

So this middle-aged bald guy tells the committee, yeah, you could say he brought in the business. But, cries D'Amato, you didn't bring in McDougal with a signed contract in hand, did you? No, says the bald guy, I didn't bring in McDougal with a signed contract in hand. Aha! cries D'Amato. And all the television networks duly run a clip of the bald guy saying, "I did not bring in McDougal with a signed contract in hand."

Well! We've certainly proved that, haven't we, Al? (I call him Al because I first knew him when he was a squirrelly pol in Long Island who used to go around saying, "Call me Al.") Al & Co. demand documents. Hillary provides documents. Al & Co. demand more documents. Hillary provides more documents. Aha! cries Al (he was always given to crying "Aha!")—why didn't you provide these documents earlier? This is sinister; there must be a plot here. (Quick, where are *your* records from fifteen years ago, and why can't you produce them all now?) Al says, "These actions raise questions about the appearance of possible improprieties." Don't you just hate that—when questions are raised about the appearance of possible improprieties?

Al has now spent about 6 million of our taxpayer dollars raising questions about the appearance of possible improprieties, but it's been worth every penny, because polls now show that 51 percent of the American people have doubts about Hillary Clinton. Good work, Al.

Personally, I'm a lot less worried about questions of the First Lady's appearance of possible improprieties than I am about D'Amato's. Hey, forget the old stuff—I mean the stuff that goes back fifteen years; who would worry about fifteen years ago, when Al testified as a character witness for a Mafia goon? (Philip Basile, described by Al as "an honest, truthful, hardworking man, a man of integrity." Al then kissed him on both cheeks, and the jury then convicted him of conspiracy to defraud and lying to the federal government.) Hey, who cares about that old stuff like D'Amato and S&L's, D'Amato and HUD, D'Amato and Roy Cohn, D'Amato and Wedtech, D'Amato and Joe Margiotta, D'Amato and junk bonds. What are you, a historian?

I'm talking about the nifty new stuff, like June 1993. Al made $37,125 in a single day on an initial stock offering made possible by a Long Island brokerage firm that at the time had serious SEC fraud charges pending against it and has since been heavily fined and sanctioned. Al was then the ranking Republican on the Banking Committee, which oversees the SEC. Al's broker at the firm bought 4,500 shares of the new stock for Al at $4 a share and sold them the same day for $12.25 a share—a deal not available to ordinary investors.

I'm talking about Al and his brother Armand. Forget Armand and the racetrack interests and all that old stuff; let's talk Armand and Unisys, late 1980s. Unisys, a Long Island defense contractor, hires Armand and pays him $120,000 to lobby for Pentagon contract business. The checks were made out to a law partner of Armand's. Armand gets Al's office to send the Navy two letters, on Al's stationery, both ghostwritten by Unisys employees, with Al's signature on them. Al was on the Defense Appropriations Committee, and the Pentagon gave Unisys a $100 million contract. Armand gets convicted of mail fraud and is sentenced to five months, out on appeal; Al gets a rebuke from the Senate Ethics Committee and never releases the documents. Appearance of possible impropriety, anyone?

Fort Worth Star-Telegram
January 21, 1996

In a GOP Never-Never Land

Be still, my heart: the single most transcendent moment of a lifetime covering politics occurred Tuesday night, and you poor schnerks in Televisionland missed it because the R's didn't have the guts to put House Speaker Newt Gingrich on during prime time.

O.K., here's what you missed (C-SPAN will be replaying this in Great Convention Moments for years to come): Gingrich explained freedom to us. It's beach volleyball.

I know, at first it's a little confusing, but follow closely. This is the new, cuddly Newt Gingrich, not the old mean Newt Gingrich. We know this because the convention video bio about him consisted of pictures of Newt being kind to little children, including a black one—not Newt kicking them off welfare or shipping them off to orphanages. We saw Newt smiling, Newt laughing, Newt with a cuddly animal, not even picking wings off flies or calling Democrats sick, disgusting traitors.

Then Newt himself appeared and started talking about freedom. Suddenly he turns to introduce this rather godlike young man wearing a gold medal slung around his neck and informs us that this is the first citizen ever to win an Olympic medal for beach volleyball. You still don't get it, but persevere.

Then Newt explains to us that beach volleyball is a game that people started playing on beaches all by themselves, without any government bureaucrats telling them how to do it. And gradually the people organized themselves into leagues and began playing competitive beach volleyball, and after twenty years they got beach volleyball accepted as an Olympic sport, all without any help from the government.

"That," said Speaker Gingrich, "is what freedom is all about."

Aaaahhh, I hear you say, *now* I understand. *Now,* for the first time, I get what freedom is all about. Yep, there it is.

Further, Newt explained, beach volleyball was accepted by the International Olympic Committee, which itself does not contain a single government bureaucrat! Leaving aside the fact that the IOC is one of the most notorious sinks of bureaucratic awfulness in the history of man, setting aside the fact that it's run by a nest of hideous old fascists (see *The Nation,* July 29–August 6), and blithely ignoring the complete lack of accountability for how the IOC spends its billions, we are to conclude that the IOC is dandy simply because it is not a *government* bureaucracy.

Nope, it's an awful snake pit of bribery, corruption, and fascists, but it is—hallelujah—a private bureaucracy. And it's so brilliantly run that various levels of government had to pony up $354 million to put on the Olympics in Atlanta, according to the *Atlanta Journal-Constitution.* And that's what freedom is all about.

This same zany conviction that nothing said here need make any sense pervades the entire convention. Bob Dole said Wednesday morning that he will increase military spending without touching Social Security or Medicare, thus completing the famous Reagan prescription for economic disaster: Cut taxes, increase spending, and the budget will balance all by itself. Promise. It's written on a napkin and called the Laffer curve.

Naturally, we all bash government here at the Republican convention, especially Washington. Government is terrible, dreadful, and awful, which is why we should vote for Dole (who has been a major player in it for thirty-six years) and Jack Kemp (for twenty-two years). Everything that's wrong with government is the fault of Bill Clinton, who first set foot outside Arkansas four years ago.

The government of the United States of America has been demonized, vilified, and used as a fire hydrant by every speaker at this convention in terms that would have made the old Soviet politburo blush, but all these folks are patriots, so it's O.K. The country is going to hell; its moral fiber is rotting; we are beset on all sides by immigrants who come here to go on welfare, murderers of unborn children, militant homosexuals, criminals, drug addicts, sex-crazed teenagers and layabouts on food stamps—*but* this is the greatest country on earth, and there is no people so generous and wonderful as ourselves.

It's hard to think of a sillier place for a major political party to take a monumentally dumb stand on immigration than San Diego. Here it stands, living proof that every argument (actually, make that every argument a Republican would make) against immigration is pure horse puckey.

San Diego is closer to Tijuana than Fort Worth is to Dallas. Although the California-Mexico border bristles with Border Patrol, bright lights, motion detectors, and other fancy, high-tech equipment, it is just as porous as Texas's own beloved border. The only difference is that no one here calls them "wets."

By day the speakers at the Republican convention inveigh against the perils of immigration; by night the litter they leave behind is cleaned up by brown-skinned people who *no habla.* As Peter King of the *Los Angeles Times* notes, the Republicans' drinks are served, their dishes are washed, their towels and sheets are changed, their toilets are cleaned, and their meals are prepared by the very people they want to boot across the border because, of course, they only come here to go on welfare.

Fort Worth Star-Telegram
August 15, 1996

Hand Social Security Over
to the Tender Mercies of
Bears and Bulls?

Let's take as a given that our government is capable of doing profoundly dumb things. These are the people who brought you the Vietnam War, the S&L crisis, the $563 hammer, the $1,200 toilet seat, the
"no-man-in-the-house" rule for welfare recipients, and the tobacco
subsidy. Not to mention the entire Civil Defense program, under
which we were to survive nuclear warfare by learning to duck and
cover.

Our government can be so dumb that many people now make a
handsome living by promoting the notion that it's a collection of
boobs who can't do anything right and shouldn't be trusted to collect
the garbage. To this end, now comes the Advisory Council on Social
Security with a monumentally dumb idea: Privatize Social Security by
investing the Social Security Trust Fund in the stock market. The first
question you want to ask about this ridiculous proposal is: Why? The
answer is: No good reason.

Social Security is one of many government programs that actually
work quite well, thank you. Since its start in 1935, Social Security has
reduced poverty in old age to less than the average for all age groups.

In addition to protecting the elderly, the program also helps middle-aged workers who would otherwise have to support their aged parents. It also acts as a giant life-insurance pool, is completely portable, and is not drained by commissions of salesmen or investment advisers.

True, we are now approaching a demographic bump in the road that presents a long-term problem for the program. Because people are living longer and the baby boomers will start to retire in fifteen years, the ratio of workers to retirees will fall to a burdensome extent. According to the council, during the next seventy-five years Social Security will be out of balance by 2.2 percent of taxable payroll.

Balance will require increases in taxes, small reductions in benefits, or some combination of both. Or we could cut benefits to wealthy retirees (Ross Perot will not miss the money) or raise the retirement age or fix the Consumer Price Index or slow cost-of-living adjustments. As you see, we have a variety of choices here to resolve a not-terribly-pressing problem—although the sooner solutions are implemented, the safer the system will be.

As the economist Robert Kuttner puts it, "Conservatives on the panel have taken the need for moderate adjustment as the occasion for fundamental change."

Social Security now collects more in taxes than it pays out in benefits. The excess—the trust fund—is invested in special U.S. Treasury bonds that paid an average of 7.6 percent last year—"not a bad return for a no-risk portfolio," noted financial writer Jane Bryant Quinn. According to Quinn, the trust fund is expected to grow until around 2019, after which it will have to start cashing in its Treasury bonds. Quinn points out that the revenues from the payroll tax alone would be enough to pay 75 percent of everyone's Social Security benefits for the next seventy-five years. A 1.1 percent increase in payroll tax for employees and employers would make up the difference, costing the average worker $23.50 a month.

Financial columnist John Crudele wrote, "If Social Security money is invested in the stock market, we can all kiss our retirements good-bye." Crudele believes that the sale of billions of dollars of government bonds in order to invest in the stock market will cause interest rates to rise dramatically. "With the government having to pay higher interest rates on its bonds, the nation's deficit will also climb signifi-cantly. When the deficit rises, investors' faith in Washington's ability to control its costs will erode and interest rates will go up some more. . . . The economy slows and corporate profits sink . . . an evil mix for the stock market."

Even assuming that this apocalyptic scenario does not play out, the risks of putting the trust fund into the stock market are still high. Be-cause of the unprecedented bull market, we seem to have forgotten that markets do come down. Judged long-term, the stock market does not offer a great improvement in profits over bonds, and it certainly poses a far greater risk. Just before this bull market, stocks declined 4 percent a year for ten years; how would you like to watch that much of your retirement savings eaten away just before you retired?

A further problem is the conflict of interest posed by a system that puts the single most influential market force, the federal government, in the position of being the single largest investor. David Sanger of *The New York Times* asks: What if a president were advised that the cost of sending troops to secure the peace on the Korean peninsula would undercut the returns that every American worker would see on his quarterly statements?

So who is in favor of this batty idea? Wall Street, of course, which is already collecting millions to promote and lobby for the change. Billions and billions of dollars suddenly flowing in would certainly fuel the stock market. If fund managers are permitted to skim just 1 percent in management fees—Sanger raises this possibility—it would mean new Wall Street revenues of $10 billion to $40 billion a year. Keep that in mind when you see glossy printed ads touting this daffy notion, or television ads giving you the hard sell on what a swell con-cept it is. Buyer, beware.

Fort Worth Star-Telegram
January 21, 1997

Welfare for Politicians—
Let's Have Reform on That

O.K., so it wasn't the Bob Bullock Memorial Award (given each session to the first member of the Texas Lege charged with drunken driving in honor of the lite gov's long-gone drinking days), but there was an interesting legislative arrest last week. State Senator Drew Nixon got himself busted on charges of soliciting a prostitute who turned out to be an undercover cop.

Scholars will recall that ere he was ever elected, Nixon was found by the Dallas police in the company of three prostitutes—but, he explained, he was only asking for directions. I find this an entirely credible defense; those who have observed Nixon in the Senate know that he frequently is completely lost.

On the other hand, there are days when Nixon looks positively bright compared with some of the rest of folks in politics. My favorite current example is U.S. Senator Fred Thompson of Tennessee, now leading the Republican charge to investigate sleazy campaign financing. Reminds me of the scene in *Blazing Saddles* where the guy puts a gun to his own head and threatens to off himself if the guys who are trying to kill him don't drop their guns.

Suppose Thompson does a good job on this investigation and exposes the entire system of legalized bribery we politely call campaign financing:

(A) The cynicism about and disgust with our political system will soar to new heights, making it ever more likely that we will turn away from both political parties and elect someone like Ross Perot.

(B) Demands for reform will mount, but Thompson is one of exactly two Republicans in the entire Senate—the other being the estimable John McCain—who actually favor campaign-finance reform. Republicans have a 2-to-1 fund-raising edge over Democrats under the current system and are not about to throw it away. Having raised the issue to new visibility, the Republicans will then have to kill it, making their electoral lives rather more difficult.

(C) Although having Thompson—a former lobbyist for major corporations and the Teamsters union pension fund—head this investigation is not quite as egregious as putting Senator Al D'Amato in charge of an ethics investigation, it ain't that far, either. According to *The Wall Street Journal,* Thompson himself has profited from hot initial public stock offerings made available to him through a politically friendly brokerage firm in Tennessee. In addition, he has a long association with Farhad Azima, a Kansas City, Missouri, businessman who was a guest at the same White House coffees we are now told were extremely sinister.

David Rogers of the *Journal* noted: "Lawmakers know their true foe is the same home-grown, corrupting, fund-raising system of which they are part. Like Pogo, they have met the enemy and it is themselves."

Meanwhile, Senate Majority Leader Trent Lott was spending three days at a luxurious, oceanfront Palm Beach resort mingling and schmoozing with fat-cat donors to the Republican party who have given at least $175,000 over four years. (Am I the only one who has noticed that Lott looks exactly like a Ford dealer? Nothing against Ford dealers, an altogether outstanding bunch, but how come they all look like Lott?) The majority leader said the big donors should be allowed to give even more because "it's the American way."

Good grief, at least President Clinton has enough sense to denounce the system while he plays it for all it's worth. Giving good sound bite, Lott added: "I support people being involved in the political process.[!] We're not for food stamps for politicians; we don't think public financing of campaigns is a good idea." [!!] And there he stood, surrounded by oilmen, insurance reps, pharmaceutical manufacturers, bankers, et cetera, et cetera.

Great green gobs of greasy, grimy gopher guts—"We're not for food stamps for politicians"??? We already *have* public financing of presidential campaigns, and this whole current furor is over the intrusion of private financing into that system. Where is this man's head?

I am for public financing of *all* campaigns, and if there were a politician in Washington with half a brain, he or she would be jumping to the head of that parade right now. I'll tell you how you sell it in a New York minute: Combine public financing with election reform. No paid political advertising, period. Time and space in the news media to be provided gratis by the media. If you take the cost of television out of campaigning, the public could finance the whole deal at pennies per person through the income tax. Frequent candidate debates during a limited time span, as in the British model.

And here's how you score political points off it. "My opponent is afraid to let our ideas and proposals compete on a level playing field. He knows perfectly well that without the advantage of special-interest money, he could never sell his pernicious notions to the American public. I don't want to go to luxurious resorts in Florida to meet my campaign contributors; I want to go to Luby's and Taco Bell and the Chat & Chew Café."

Sheesh, where's a demagogue when you need one?

Fort Worth Star-Telegram
February 23, 1997

Upholding the
Political Reputation of
the Lone Star State

My, my, my, our Texas boys in Washington are certainly distinguish-
ing themselves these days, aren't they? Our boy Tom DeLay, the
House minority whip and former exterminator from Sugar Land,
added luster to our reputation for gentle manners and civilized behavior by shoving a congressman from Wisconsin on the House floor and
apostrophizing him as "a gutless chickenshit." Now they know: Not
everyone from Sugar Land is sweet.

DeLay's spokesman said afterward that the Texan got so upset because the fellow from Wisconsin questioned his integrity and DeLay
is not accustomed to having his integrity questioned. Well, if he's not,
he should be, since it's been going on for quite some time now.

In fact, the newspaper article the Wisconsin fellow was carrying on
about is more than two years old. That's the story about DeLay having
had a bunch of lobbyists in his office rewriting federal regulations.

Then there was the story about DeLay's putting the arm on lobbyists for contributions; that's why they call him "the Hammer" in D.C.
And the stories about DeLay's brother the lobbyist and how DeLay
carries water for him. DeLay, as a former exterminator, also thinks that

pesticides are wonderful and that we should bring back DDT, although this has led more people to question his sanity than his integrity.

Our boy Dick Armey from Irving, the House majority leader, is also in the news, illustrating a nice point about argumentation. As the Republican leadership vowed to extirpate the National Endowment for the Arts both root and branch, Armey said: "I object to those who say that without a government agency we are cultural idiots." I cannot swear that no one has ever referred to Armey as a cultural idiot, but I do know that is not the line of reasoning used by those in favor of the NEA.

This is a perfect example of a rhetorical trick that gets us into many stupid arguments and entrenched positions—that is, when a person on one side of an issue defines not only his view but that of his opponents as well. When you redefine what your opponents believe, it's amazing how often it sounds like drivel. I know; I have stooped to this trick myself on occasion, but it is a nasty device.

By misstating what people who disagree with you think about almost anything, you can make your position look ever so much more reasonable and inviting. But this is not a helpful device; it just gets people stuck in knee-jerk positions and draws attention away from the merits of the arguments on either side.

The other day a talking head on television declared: "The feminists have been lying to us for twenty years; they say women should be just like men." Oh, piffle. I have been a feminist for thirty-five years and have never heard anyone say any such thing.

What feminists say is that women should get equal pay for equal work; and believe it or not, that has been a long, hard struggle. We also believe that women should have more opportunities than was common in the past—opportunities to be doctors as well as nurses, pilots as well as stewardesses, executives as well as secretaries, and certainly full-time mothers if they choose to be.

Back in D.C., Our Boy Bill Archer from Houston, chairman of the House Ways and Means Committee, is about to come onstage in a big way. Speaker Newt Gingrich has decided to start a major offensive to get both the capital-gains tax and the estate tax eliminated, which will put Our Boy Bill in the spotlight, making what I believe is a sorry case. The usual disinformation is already circulating.

"Why should the government take 55 percent of everything you make in your lifetime?" demanded an indignant John Sununu. Good question, except that the government doesn't do that. Estate taxes do not even apply to those who leave under $600,000; to get into the 55 percent bracket, you have to leave millions, and people who have millions to leave use "estate planners" to avoid paying taxes.

The argument on capital gains, unearned income, is even more bizarre. Two thirds of the money that comes from the capital-gains tax is paid by people who are rich even by Republican standards. Finding them arguing furiously for their right to unearned income is a curious sight indeed. It always reminds me of Henry George's nineteenth-century proposal for a single tax, on real estate: George argued that since the only reason real estate ever increases in value is because of the community (as the community grows, so do real estate values), all real estate profits properly belong to the community.

The Republicans argue that the capital-gains tax discourages investment. We've noticed how discouraged investors are lately. Scarcely a nickel can the poor stock market find because of that nasty capital-gains tax.

Well, I often say to people from Washington who question what we send up there: You should see what we've got back home.

Fort Worth Star-Telegram
April 13, 1997

The Only Prez We've Got
Should Stand and Fight

Bill Clinton, as Lyndon was fond of reminding us about himself in his day, is the only president we've got. And Clinton is the Rodney Dangerfield of presidents.

He is so constantly and so casually abused, vilified, dismissed, mocked, and generally treated as a punching bag by every snide little twerp with a press pass that it's a little startling to realize that his approval ratings continue to ride in the mid-50s. Wouldn't guess that from reading the papers, would you?

On the wilder shores of talk radio and the paranoid-right press, Clinton is regularly accused of murder, drug dealing, and any number of lesser crimes. A substantial minority of the citizenry seems to be prepared to believe he sucks eggs, runs on all fours, and molests small children—which is especially odd in that his single most striking public attribute is his eternal niceness.

In the five years of his presidency—during which time he has had a Rocky Mountain range of abuse heaped on his head—we have seen him respond somewhat curtly exactly twice. The other day in Mexico he answered two unpleasant questions about his wife by saying quietly, "No and no," and then he shut his mouth and tightened his lips. This titanic eruption of volcanic temper caused a great twittering in Washington.

That's pretty much how it goes for Clinton. If there is one single thing he has done or failed to do that has not been viciously criticized, I wish you would point it out to me. He has been criticized for dumping his friends when they get in trouble and for not dumping his friends when they get in trouble. First he was accused of trying to do too much; now he's accused of trying to do too little. He's criticized for bashing Republicans; he's criticized for working with Republicans. The man can't even promote volunteerism without being criticized.

All of which sets off my contrarian impulses. I frankly don't care about his sex life; I don't think it's any of my business. Nor do I care about the stupid land deal he got into in 1978; have you ever seen so much fuss made about so little in your life? If Clinton were personally corrupt, he'd be rich by now. As Sid Richardson once said of John Connally, "We just put him in the way to make a little money." That's how it's done for politicians who are interested in acquiring wealth. I'd say Clinton is not, and I'd say the proof is his bank account.

Politically corrupt? Yes, I think so. But then you get into thornier issues, such as: Compared to whom? Is the problem Clinton, or is it the system? They're all in hock to big contributors; is it worse to let rich folks buy a night in the Lincoln Bedroom or to let them rewrite environmental regulations? If it is sleazy beyond redemption for Clinton to take money from a foreign businessman through a shell corporation, then it's just as sleazy for the Republicans, who did it as well.

Yeah, I'd like to kick 'em all out, but I think it would be more useful to completely change the campaign-financing system—and put an end to paid political ads while we're at it. At least Clinton supports changing the campaign-financing laws, which is more than can be said for the R's.

In many ways, Clinton is the most skilled politician I've ever watched work. I know it's ridiculous to complain about a politician behaving like a politician—fish gotta swim and politicians gotta deal—but my problem with him is simply that. Too much politician in him; not enough leader, not enough fighter. He's starting his endgame now, and I believe that both Garry Kasparov and Deep Blue would tell him it's time to change tactics.

You can't get a decent deal with people who don't *want* the government to work. They don't want it to work well; they don't want it to work at all. The Shiite Republicans aren't interested in fixing government—they want to destroy it.

Why let them? Why let them abolish the tax credit for investing in low-income housing when we continue to subsidize housing for Donald Trump, who gets to write off the interest on his family mansion, his New York condo, his place in the country, his villa in Aspen, his townhouse in Miami, and his grand estate in Palm Beach? Why cut the capital-gains tax and the estate tax (so rich folks will invest more, explain the R's) when the R's aren't willing to invest even $5 billion of the $112 billion needed to repair schools in this country? You tell me what's a better investment.

I think Clinton should give up on trying to make deals with these folks and just start kicking ass. And do we think he will? Of course not. Pol to the bone.

Fort Worth Star-Telegram
May 11, 1997

Not Many Winners in
This Can of Worms

As one of the leading rooters in the Feminists for Paula Jones camp, let me say how pleased we are by the Supremes' decision in our case last week.

Simple principal: No one's above the law. O.K., if in the future this turns out to be a means of harassing a sitting president by his political enemies, then, maybe then, Congress may want to consider an executive form of a common practice—the "legislative continuance." For example, members of the Texas Legislature get a pass on all their legal involvements while the Lege is in session. It doesn't put them above the law; it just means their bidness is postponed until the session is over.

Of course, the Lege only meets for 140 days once every other year, as opposed to a potential eight years for a president, which gets you into the speedy-trial thicket. That would have to be balanced against the Lege's important work in naming the state chili pepper, as opposed to whatever a president might have on his or her plate.

But for the nonce, Our Girl, as we think of her, has won a major victory for just plain folks, and we rejoice. This is particularly sweet, given all the classist abuse she has had to take, much from our fellow feminists and even more from my fellow journalists.

Shall we ever forget the time Our Girl posed for a *Newsweek* cover wearing a nice blue angora sweater, only to have every snippy little snob with a press pass denounce her as "tacky." You would think we would have gotten a break from the natural-fibers crowd on that one, but no, in their eyes, blue eye shadow is only slightly less heinous than child molestation. Anyone who thinks there's no such thing as a class system in America need only look at the treatment given Our Girl.

Now that Ms. Jones has Supreme permission to proceed with our case, the original problem of whether we actually have a case reappears. I'm afraid our lawyer Gilbert Davis didn't help when he said: "Paula Jones wants her name and good reputation back from Bill Clinton. He's got it, she wants it and we're going to get it for her."

Er, ah, ahem. We will have to stipulate, as the lawyers say, that it was not Clinton who took away Jones's good name. Whether you believe him or you believe her, for obvious reasons he never said a word about her. If it had been left to Clinton, Jones's reputation would be as unsullied as Mother Teresa's. Our lawyer was a little over the top there.

Now, it can be argued that people associated with Clinton have trashed Jones. In fact, James Carville, Clinton's 1992 campaign manager, once referred to her as "trailer trash," an epithet at which I took particular umbrage. I have friends who live in trailers. However, Carville was not working for Clinton at that point and hadn't been for some time, and it is difficult to believe that Clinton ordered him to pop off. Carville has, on his record, never been much under anyone's control. His wife often says so. If the "trailer trash" crack is what stung, our beef is with Carville, not Clinton.

As for the media's reportage of the unpleasant comments made by some of Our Girl's kinfolk, well, it is my belief that we all have unfortunate relatives. But that's not Clinton's fault either.

The fact is that no one in the larger world would know a single thing about Our Girl's reputation had she not called a news conference and announced that she was filing this case. Her name had never appeared in the public prints; no one knew or cared who she was. It was three years after the alleged incident, and in all that time she had never considered filing suit.

All this transpired as follows: An anti-Clinton crusader named David Brock printed in a tiny, anti-Clinton magazine the allegation by a fired state trooper guilty of fraud that a woman named Paula wanted to be Clinton's "regular girlfriend." Lot of Paulas in the world. But Our Girl felt she had been outed, as it were—damage to her reputation, the whole nine yards—and filed suit. Oddly enough, she did not sue Brock, the magazine, or the trooper.

Our case, *qua* case, rests not merely on what happened in the Hotel Excelsior office room between Clinton and Jones but on *whether there were any adverse consequences to Jones's employment because of it.* In other words, as the law says, the creation of a hostile work environment. Here's where we have our problem. After the alleged incident, Our Girl got both promotions and pay raises. Now she says her work was adversely affected—perhaps she should have gotten *more* promotions and pay raises—but she didn't say so at the time. This is where I fear our case is a trifle weak.

Meanwhile, all this leaves the citizenry, not to mention the president, in a rather unpleasant pickle. From the point of view of justice, this is a tale of *Rashomon* (a classic Japanese film on the slippery nature of truth).

For a while it looked as though Our Girl, with the power of the presidency arrayed against her, would never get a fair hearing. Now the question arises as to whether Clinton, with the power of public humiliation arrayed against him, can afford to go through a trial. Even if he is found not guilty of sexual harassment—as seems likely, given the aforementioned weakness in our case—the damage to his reputation, concentration, and ability to function in office will be massive. None of that is Our Girl's fault.

But the question does arise, once again: What kind of lawyers advised Our Girl to bring a lawsuit with such a dubious chance of success that would so evidently harm both him and her? Who were these lawyers, and what were their motives?

The answer is they were ideological zealots who wanted to get Clinton for political reasons, and at least one of them looked for movie and TV deals before filing the suit. Cliff Jackson, a Little Rock lawyer who has spent years trying to destroy Clinton, first brought Jones to Washington to make her allegation before the Conservative Political Action Committee. Her first lawyer, Daniel Traylor, approached a friend of Clinton's and told him that Jones would settle for an apology, financial compensation, and jobs for herself and her husband. Another lawyer who volunteered to help was Ken Starr, now special prosecutor in the Whitewater case.

I believe that Our Girl has been used and abused by more than one man in this mess.

Fort Worth Star-Telegram
June 3, 1997

Boring?
I Don't Think So

Aw, gee. The Washington press corps thinks the campaign-finance hearings are a bore. No bombshells. No sex. Bad story line. Chairman Fred Thompson may be an actor by profession, but he can't write dialogue worth squat. Call a script doctor.

I'm so sorry the press finds this boring. Too bad it's not up to our high standards of entertainment. On the other hand, we might consider sharing with the American people that these hearings are semi-important, whether they're sexy or not. Instead of critiquing the performances of the players, we might remind people what this is about. The corruption of the American political system. The root of the rot. The source of everything that is wrong with our political life. The reason our democratic system is in peril. The reason politicians no longer represent the people.

The truth is that there is no political story more important than campaign financing. It's not just the hottest political story—it's the only story. It's the key to the real source of the class warfare in this country.

Congress passed a minimum-wage increase last year. You remember that—an increase of (TA-DA! TA-DA!) 90¢, all the way up to $5.15 an hour for eleven million Americans, two thirds of them adults, most of them trying to support families. And when the bill was finally passed amidst much back-patting, lo, we looked closely and found it also contained $21 *billion* worth of corporate giveaways.

Here are just a few of those items, taken from Jim Hightower's forthcoming book, *Nothing in the Middle of the Road But Yellow Stripes and Dead Armadillos:*

- A "clarification" of tax law allows newspaper conglomerates to classify their carriers—the minimum-wage folks who bring your morning paper—as "independent contractors." This allows the Murdochs, Dealys, Coxes, Hearsts, Ridders, and other billionaire publishers to avoid paying Social Security, unemployment, and other benefits to those folks who are hailed in the annual editorials on Newspaper Carriers Day.

- U.S. multinationals snuck on an amendment eliminating taxes on income they make from their foreign factories. A little incentive to move more factories and jobs overseas, wouldn't you say?

- Corporate raiders—guys like Henry Kravis, Ron Perelman, and others who conduct hostile takeovers of corporations and then fire the employees and plunder the assets of takeover targets—got a great big goodie, too. These folks pay billions of dollars in fees to investment bankers to finance their job-destroying raids, but now, thanks to a "technical correction" in the minimum-wage bill, those fees will be *tax-deductible.* Even better, Congress made the tax deductibility retroactive!

And all that happened because of our campaign-financing system. All of that is about money donated to politicians by large special interests.

"Oh, but the people aren't interested in campaign financing," the press is now whining. "They're on vacation. They're following the stock market instead. These hearings just *don't affect their lives.*" Oh yeah? Well let me suggest that we get them interested. We could call it the Cynthia Chavez Wall Memorial Effort.

Cynthia Chavez Wall was a single mother who worked for a textile factory near Hamlet, North Carolina, for thirteen years. She was making $8 an hour until she was abruptly fired for not coming to work one day; instead, she stayed home to take care of her daughter, who had pneumonia.

Desperate for a job, she hired on at Imperial Food Processors at $4.95 an hour. She cut and prepared chicken parts sold in fast-food restaurants. She often went home with her hands bleeding from cuts she inevitably got trying to keep pace with the constant demands to speed up the process. She worked next to oil vats heated to 400 degrees—no air-conditioning, no fans, only a few small windows.

Then one day, flames and smoke started to billow through the building, which had no sprinkler system, no evacuation plan, and only one fire extinguisher. As the fire spread, people panicked and ran to the exit doors. All but the front doors had been padlocked from the outside.

Company executives later explained that they did this to prevent chicken parts from being stolen. Twenty-five of the ninety workers in the building died that day; more than fifty others were burned or injured. The body of Cynthia Chavez Wall was found by one of the locked doors.

Terrible accident? Not once in eleven years had that building been inspected for safety—although Ag Department employees came to check on the quality of the chicken meat. Earlier that year, the North Carolina Legislature voted against toughening up the state's safety regs; the average workplace there is inspected once every seventy-five years. Due to cuts during the Reagan and Bush administrations, the federal government now has 1,200 inspectors to cover 7 million American workplaces.

Two years after Cynthia Wall died, when all the media and politicians had gone away again, a private group went back to inspect the chicken plants in Hamlet. Assembly-line speedups still cause injuries; stifling heat and oppressive working conditions still remain; ill and injured employees must stay on the line or be fired. And the doors are still locked from the outside.

That is a story about the effects of our campaign-financing system. Hope it didn't bore you too much.

Fort Worth Star-Telegram
July 15, 1997

Texas Culture
and Politics

Some Kind of Christian

Since the fundamentalists keep describing this as "a Christian nation" and insisting that that's what the founders intended it to be, I'd really like to get their opinion on the matter of the sale of "death futures" on AIDS victims. And I can think of few better people to ask than state representative Warren Chisum of Pampa, that well-known crusader against homosexuality, who also happens to be an investor in death futures.

Chisum could not be reached for this column, but he told *The Houston Post* last month that profits on death futures run up to a 27 percent rate of return, which apparently covers all his Christian scruples. Chisum now owns life-insurance policies on six AIDS victims—a $200,000 investment. "My gamble is that it'll make not less than 17 percent and sometimes considerably better," Chisum told the *Post.* "If they die in one month, you know, they do really good."

The trade in death futures is one of the more esoteric wrinkles of advanced capitalism. Investors pay terminally ill patients 50 percent to 80 percent of the actual value of their life-insurance policies. The AIDS patients get some money to make their lives more comfortable and to pay for their medicine for a while, and the investors get the full value of the policies after the victims die. This charming new industry is known as "viatical settlements," and there are now fifty companies trading in this commodity nationwide.

AIDS support groups back this trade on the grounds that many dying patients need the money. In fact, state representative Glen Maxey cosponsored a death-futures bill in the Texas Legislature with Chisum in order, he said, to bring the trade under the regulation of the state Department of Insurance. Maxey, as the press always tediously points out, is "the only openly gay member of the Legislature."

Chisum has voted against expanding foster care for babies with AIDS and a variety of other programs to help AIDS victims. He even opposed the hate-crimes bill because it would cover gays, and he opposes sex education "because most sex education they've been trying to have is promotion of the homosexual lifestyle." Sex education is the most effective way to prevent the spread of AIDS.

So here we have someone shaping public policy who has an open monetary interest in seeing that the epidemic continues and that no cure is found. By his own votes, he has helped to ensure that.

Different Christians have different standards, of course. For myself, I'd rather die of AIDS than report to my maker after doing what Chisum is doing.

Fort Worth Star-Telegram
March 16, 1994

Sometimes I think I made Warren Chisum up for my own amusement.

Brother Chisum, the Bible-thumper from Pampa and chairman of the Legislature's conservative caucus, is opposing a bill to require that caucuses report who gives them money and how the money is spent, even though last session he headed the committee that recommended the same law. State representative Chisum says some of the people who have contributed to his caucus don't want it known. "We will never disclose those. Everybody else, we are happy to disclose."

Thank you, Brother Chisum. One of the recurring features of covering the Texas Legislature is the desire to keep saying, "Excuse me, I think I have a banana in my ear. Do what?"

Chisum often induces this reaction. One of his better bills this session would prohibit state agencies from considering the environment when choosing fuel. Yes, Chisum believes that considering the environment should be prohibited by law. If the environment should happen to cross your mind while you are trying to decide between leaded, unleaded, diesel, or gasohol, severe legal penalties would ensue.

The phrase "the common good" is not in Chisum's working vocabulary. He is, however, hell-bent on making sex education about abstinence. He has introduced a five-part bill that would require any course in human sexuality to (1) present abstinence; (2) devote substantially more attention to abstinence from sexual activity than to any other behavior; (3) emphasize abstinence; (4) direct adolescents to abstinence; and (5) teach contraception and condom use in terms of human-use reality rates instead of theoretical laboratory rates. (Just take the banana out of your ear.)

Fort Worth Star-Telegram
February 9, 1995

Travels with the Bard

We were having the most soporific yawner of a Senate race here in Texas—we have to replace Lloyd Bentsen—when it just now got interesting. Texans are accustomed to brawls, duke-outs, and generally peppy politics, but the firestorm of boredom engulfing the less-than-titanic contest between Kay Bailey Hutchison, a carefully moderate-by-Texas-standards Republican, and Bob Krueger, an adequate Democrat, threatened to rage out of control.

Hutchison was well ahead on points, having skunked two congressmen, one a real right-winger and the other a sort of television weathercaster specimen, in the first elimination round. She actually finished a hair ahead of Krueger, who was appointed to the Bentsen seat by Governor Ann Richards for reasons no one understands, except that Henry Cisneros was not available. Hutchison is state treasurer and has a solid record because her predecessor in that office, the same Ann Richards, set up a good shop. Krueger was a railroad commissioner, a misnomer having to do with oil and gas regulation, an office that ain't worth dog since the oil crash. He had also lost twice before, trying for the Senate. No one could quite remember why until he started running again and we were all reminded that he's militantly anticharismatic.

For quite a while, Hutchison was the only fun—she claimed she spoke Spanish, and when challenged to say something in that language, she replied, "Nolo contendere." Then John Connally's daughter claimed that when she was working for Hutchison at the Treasury, Hutchison lost her temper and hit her on the shoulder several times with a ring binder. Hutchison indignantly denied it. A flap ensued over why women running for public office always get accused of having bad tempers.

In the excitement, Connally's daughter's other charges—that she had been required to work on Hutchison's house on state time—got lost in the shuffle.

Meanwhile, Krueger—who used to teach literature at Duke University—was being Krueger, much to everyone's dismay. Two politically prominent persons went on a campaign swing with him. The first stop was Beaumont. One politically prominent person said to the other, "If Krueger quotes Shakespeare here, I'm gonna kill him."

Krueger did, of course, work the Bard into his speech to oil-field workers. They went on to San Antonio, where Krueger quoted Dante. The second politically prominent person said to the first, "You're not gonna kill him. I am."

Personally, I especially enjoyed the day he quoted Plutarch in Midland and another occasion in San Antonio on which he informed an interested audience of union workers that *integritas* is the Latin for "integrity."

Having listened to the hopelessly literate Krueger make a painful effort to use the Texas expression "that ol' dog won't hunt," I made up a crib sheet for him in which several Texas expressions were translated into Shakespeare. For example, "How the cow ate the cabbage" becomes "Mark how yon horn-crown'd, three-stomach'd beast doth feast upon the furled green that hath for so long stunketh up the castle keep."

It didn't help.

A no-hoper. Krueger has bad hair, bad suits, a face like a potato, and an incurably learned mind. So his political consultants decided to throw long. Let Krueger be Krueger. If you've got lemons, make lemonade. His new ad starts, "I'm Bob Krueger, the guy who finished second in the race for my own Senate seat. So what was it? The hair? The suit? My Arnold Schwarzenegger physique? . . . Wasn't it Shakespeare who said, 'Hasta la vista, baby'?"

The new ads brag on his political klutziness with man-in-the-street interviews:

"Who's just awful at being a politician?"

"Must be Bob Krueger."

"Who quotes Willie Shakespeare instead of Willie Nelson?"

"Definitely, Bob Krueger."

No one knows if the ads will work, but they've produced the first spark of interest in the race so far.

Meanwhile, the Texas Legislature continues to distinguish itself. The public schools are about to be shut down because of our unconstitutional school-financing system, so the Lege decided to pass a concealed-handgun bill, you see. Don't ask. They've also managed to criminalize massage therapy for horses and kitty shrinks. Don't ask. And with any luck at all, we'll finally get a state arts fund paid for with a tax on jockstraps. You must admit, that would be excellent.

The Progressive
July 1993

Impersonating the Lord

We're having trouble again with that fellow who runs around impersonating the Lord. This cad, claiming to be God, told the Rodriguez family of Floydada, Texas, last month that if they didn't get naked, get in their car, and drive to Louisiana, he, God, would destroy Floydada (which is, incidentally, pronounced "Floy-*day*-da," *not* like the art movement).

Now, you know perfectly well that wasn't really God. Someone was just funnin' the Rodriguezes. God might destroy Floydada sometime, on aesthetic grounds, but He'd never tell anyone to go to Louisiana.

The upshot of this deplorable case of Lord impersonation was that the entire Rodriguez family, buck naked, drove to Vinton, Louisiana, Marcia Ball's hometown, where they were startled by a cop, drove into a tree, and then twenty nekkid folks piled out of a GTO (five kids in the trunk), which just astonished the hell out of the Vinton cops. The driver was incarcerated, the other Rodriguezes were remanded to the care of the Baptist church in nearby Sulphur, Louisiana, and the Vinton cops still haven't recovered.

I figure this Lord impersonator is the same guy who pulled that prank on Oral Roberts a few years back. Remember when Roberts said that God had told him to tell us, "Pay up or the preacher gets it"? Same joker. You notice he's concentrating on the Texas-Oklahoma area. I won't deny that we have an unusually high percentage of geeks in this neck of the prairie because, let's face it, we do. But I don't think it's fair for this prankster to be pickin' on our geeks.

I think the Texas Lege should pass a bill making impersonatin' the Lord a felony and then we should have a kind of neighborhood watch, with everyone callin' in suspected cases of Lord impersonation to the Texas Rangers.

I don't see why God should take the blame when preachers or citizens claim they've heard from him and then say somethin' idiotic. They can say it on their own, like my old preacher, who once observed, "My friends, to be a good Christian, you must, uuhhh, be a good Christian."

Governor Ann Richards spent the summer getting her motorcycle license so she can ride this dreamy white bike the Harley-Davidson company sent her, even though she had to donate it to the Highway Patrol because she can't take gifts. She has a hard time getting her hair into her helmet. She says the real reason she vetoed the concealed-handgun bill—a lot of people said it would make women feel safer if they could carry a handgun in their purse—is: "You *know* I am not a sexist, but I don't know a woman in this world who could *find* a gun in her handbag."

While the guv and I are on the subject of World Betterment, one result of this summer is that we think it should be against the law for radio and television weathercasters to announce "temperatures in the low one hundreds" in a perky tone of voice. Sounding lugubrious should be mandatory when one is announcing a temperature in the low 100s.

I have a friend who has just returned from Djibouti on the Gulf of Aden, so now I know how to pronounce it. And my next suggestion for World Betterment is that the ruler of that city should be a prince called Sheik Djibouti. Yours for General Improvement.

The Progressive
October 1993

Lubbock in My Rearview Mirror? Perish the Thought!

LUBBOCK, TEXAS — The dateline might as well read Bliss, Paradise, or Elysium because, of course, I love Lubbock madly. Sometimes people look at me funny when I say that, but only because they don't know Lubbock. For instance, one of the local television stations just ran a three-part investigative series on panty hose. Called *Born to Run.*

The reason you know I'm not making this up is because no one could.

There's lots of good news in the Queen City of the Plains, or, as it is sometimes written, Plain. Lubbock now has a cultural center because a local seed-and-feed dealer named Godbold put up the money for it, and a fine cultural center it is, too. The Godbold Center has an espresso and cappuccino bar, so there; let's not hear any more animadversions on Lubbock culture—except they have to get a better statue of Buddy Holly; this one appears to be made out of bubble gum.

Politically, Lubbock's unfortunate tendency toward conservatism has reached such a pass that even people like the county clerk, who's been getting elected as a Democrat since shortly after the earth's crust cooled, switched parties this year. Mark Harmon, who is running unopposed for Democratic county chairman, says he's thinking of switching parties so he can get elected, too.

Like all places in West Texas, Lubbock sometimes feels sorry for itself because it's on the wrong side of the Interstate 35 Curtain, and everyone knows West Texas has no political clout these days. Except that Lubbock just happens to have this Murderer's Row line-up in the Lege: House Speaker Pete Laney is from Hale Center, which is practically exurban Lubbock, and John Montford, the last living Democrat out here, is chair of the senate finance committee and a perennial on the Ten Best list—some would even say he's the One Best. On top of which, Rob Junell of San Angelo, chair of the house appropriations committee, and Bob Bullock, the single most powerful person in state government, are both Tech grads, which is why Tech is about to join UT and A & M in the Big Eight—it is not because of the Red Raiders' football record.

Despite farmers' having quite a good year, one local fellow decided to mow a political message into his wheat field: the name *Clinton* with a bar through it. According to yet another local television news reporter, the fellow made the message "with his concubine."

The big political battle in Lubbock is over District Attorney Travis Ware, who has (ahem) been acting strangely in the opinion of some. Ware was caught up in the messy scandal about the incompetent medical examiner, which caused all those bodies to be dug up and much other awkwardness a year ago.

Lubbock's other great contribution to political bizarreness is Monte Hasie, who for some reason is on the State Board of Education, where he runs around sighting evidence of witchcraft in school textbooks and demanding that it be removed. (If talking animals are evidence of witchcraft, is Kermit the Frog a warlock?)

I'm working on a theory that there may actually be a scientific explanation for why Texas is so strange. We know there's helium in the air in Amarillo, there's lithium in the water in El Paso, and in Lubbock and environs, there's so much mineral in the water that everyone's teeth get real strong and yellow. (This is the subject of Robin

Dorsey's famous country song, "Her Teeth Was Stained But Her Heart Was Pure." The water has been known to kill goldfish and African violets. Don't you think it's likely that whatever it is that makes yellow teeth has some effect on the old psyche as well? Of course, in East Texas, we'll just have to accept that the problem is genetic. And if there is some natural element responsible for South Texas, we probably don't want to know about it.

In an interesting historical footnote, I met the son-in-law of one of the people responsible for the first environmental action ever taken in the Great State. Few are alive who still recall this epoch-making event, but it was right here in Lubbock that the Texas environmental movement got started. Over a feedlot, of course. This particular feedlot stank so bad that even feedlot-hardened Lubbockians complained. So the City Council, in its majestic wisdom, decided to solve the problem by putting a bottle of Airwick up on every fence post around the feedlot. The son-in-law informs me that the feedlot owner later invited all the Airwick protesters over for dinner and gave each of the ladies a bottle of Chanel No. 5. I find this Lubbockian.

Fort Worth Star-Telegram
February 27, 1994

It's Been a Quiet Month
at the Capitol . . .

Metaphor of the Month comes from state senator David Sibley of Waco, heretofore unsung in the ranks of legislative phrasemakers. The extreme difficulty of trying to write tort-reform legislation, Sibley said, makes it comparable to "playing pickup sticks with your butt cheeks—no matter what you do, you mess up everything."

For aptness, for vividness, this ranks up with some of the great Gibberisms uttered by former House speaker Gib Lewis. Always nice to see new rhetorical talent emerging at the Lege. Especially since little else is.

The Lege is stuck with reruns this session. We have gone from Son of Tort Reform Bill to Great-Grandson of Tort Reform. We are on Son of Concealed Weapons Law, Son of Vegetable Libel, Son of Hate Crimes, et cetera. It's a been-there, done-that kind of session.

In an effort to find a new issue, Representatives Warren Chisum and Bob Hunter have got into a skunk match over whether the longhorn or the armadillo should be the state mammal. Representative Richard Raymond of Benavides is pushing a proposal that would make the prickly pear cactus the official vegetable-fruit of Texas. Why not? We already have a state reptile and a state seashell.

Passions are running low; even First Amendment absolutists get tired of explaining to legislators why making it illegal to disparage an agricultural product (the vegetable libel law) is unconstitutional. More imagination is required. Let's get ex-President George Bush up here to stand up for his right to trash broccoli.

God, gays, and guns are always good for some excitement. Representative Keith Oakley of Terrell is finding out firsthand what fun the gun nuts are: "A guy with Peaceable Texans for Guns called me the other day to say he was going to kill me."

And Oakley *favors* concealed weapons, but he wants to let people vote in a referendum on whether to allow them, instead of just passing a law to make it legal. Those of us who are actually against concealed weapons—on the quaint theory that the last thing this state needs is more nincompoops with guns wandering around—get lots of death threats. This does not inspire us with confidence that the average citizen can be safely allowed to tote concealed weapons.

The Fort Worth vigilante group Dead Serious is offering $5K to any member who plugs a criminal—precisely the kind of people who prove that allowing people to carry concealed handguns is not a smart idea. All you have to do is hear the barely suppressed rage in these people's voices to know they really should not be carrying guns. They're shoot-firsters, which means we're going to get a lot of dead kids who were just trying to get their baseballs back off someone else's property.

The egregious Representative Chisum is once more trying to get gays taken out of coverage under the hate-crimes bill because, he says, gays bring violence on themselves. The *Austin American-Statesman* quoted Chisum as saying, "They go to parks and pick up men, and they don't know if that someone is gay or not." Sure. Right.

There is hope, though. A visiting minister offered this invocation for Texas senators recently: "Father, I pray for these men and women.

You know how much they need it. They are facing problems that are much too immense for them to handle alone. They are not smart enough, nor do they have the capacity. I ask that you would do miracles for them."

Fort Worth Star-Telegram
February 23, 1995

Texas Liberals Ought to Come in Tablet Form

Ah, nothing like a few restful weeks contemplating the decline of civilization to restore the humors. What I did on my summer vacation was listen to a lot of people talk about the decline of practically everything—you could call it the leisure of the theory class.

I'm especially taken with *The Atlantic Monthly*'s contention that our nation has the psyche of an adolescent male—the Beavis-and-Butthead–ization of America. Only those who have fourteen-year-old males in their families know what a truly terrifying concept this is. However, a law of accounting for the decline of practically everything is that no theory is complete unless it blames both television and Ronald Reagan, who was more in the Howdy Doody tradition than in the Beavis-and-Butthead school.

After much listening and pondering, I have come to this conclusion: What our country needs is more Texas liberals.

Before you accuse me of hopeless parochialism, consider the one great truth that all Texas liberals grasp in their cradles: Things Can Always Get Worse. In fact, they often do. Therefore, it is incumbent upon us to rejoice now, because these will probably turn out to be the Good Old Days.

Can you imagine how embarassed Rush Limbaugh's callers are going to be?

"Dad, what did you do in the Good Old Days?"

"Well, son, I called radio talk shows and kvetched, gritched, moaned, and whined about how terrible everything was."

The pride of Texas liberals is that we remain of good cheer in the face of adversity—adversity being, as near as we can tell, the natural order of things. So resolved are we to enjoy things before they get worse that we consider it an imperative to Have Fun.

Texas liberals mostly have fun by gathering a mess of beer, guitars, dogs, and good folks, and plonking ourselves somewhere outdoors in the Great State so we can get sunburned and bitten by mosquitoes, fleas, ticks, chiggers, tarantulas, brown recluse spiders, and all four varieties of poisonous snakes found on the North American continent. Now you understand why people who consider this fun are so desperately needed on the national level. Any situation that doesn't include all these ingredients can only be More Fun.

The other great rule of Texas liberalism is: It doesn't matter what happens, as long as you can get a good story out of it. Thus our campfires resound not only with tales of true Texas heroes but with gleeful paeans to the delicious wrongheadedness of the Goober and the Gibber, Poor Ol' Preston and Dollar Bill Clements, Goose Finnell and Snake Nugent, the Unspeakable Hollowell and the Wrong Don Yarbrough, the Bull of the Brazos, Pass-the-Biscuits-Pappy O'Daniel and Mad Dog Mengden. We have to *appreciate* these people because we may not see their like again, and then where will we be for good stories?

"Hell, I miss George Parr," said David Richards the other night.* You see? Americans are worrying about the wrong stuff. The looming villain shortage is given no attention on the national level.

---

* George Parr, the late Duke of Duval County, was a certified son of a bitch.

All these fools in Washington sit around decrying partisanship and calling for more bipartisanship. Poop. What we need in this country is two political parties, and what we're getting is one—the party of what FDR called the Malefactors of Great Wealth. One brilliant analysis out of Washington recently explained why Interior Secretary Bruce Babbitt is a failure: He made the mistake, said the pundit, of taking on the lumber companies *and* the mining companies *and* the corporate ranchers all at once. This is not a mistake. This is a hero. So now timber, mining, and corporate ranching have ganged up on Babbitt and are pushing him back. So *push them back.*

The new vogue in politics is virtue; Bill Bennett carries the flag for the politics of virtue for the Republicans and Hillary Rodham Clinton for the Democrats. It's all such bull. Politics in this country isn't about left and right; it's about up and down. The few are screwing the many.

Even Wright Patman once admitted that not all of our most powerful and influential citizens are greedy. Some perfectly nice people are stinking rich, and being poor seldom gives people better manners. But as Patman also said, it's perfectly natural that powerful and wealthy people seek more power, more influence, and greater wealth. We call that greed. The trouble is that they have no vision. And the Bible says, where there is no vision, the people perish.

Liberty and justice for all ain't likely in my lifetime or yours, but we're sure not going to make much progress toward it if we spend all our time complaining because we're not there yet. So take a lesson from Texas liberals: Rejoice and take joy in the now. And remember: Guns don't kill killdee—people kill killdee.*

Fort Worth Star-Telegram
September 8, 1994

---

* This is a reference to an unfortunate moment in George W. Bush's gubernatorial campaign: Bush went dove-hunting, an obligatory photo op to Texas pols, and proudly showed off his kill—a protected bird called the killdee.

The Perils of Pauline's
Legal Aid in South Texas

BERKELEY, CALIFORNIA — Texas Rural Legal Aid has the starring role in a perpetual performance of *The Perils of Pauline.* ("And he tied her to the railroad tracks again!") The villain in this perennial saga is always the same and has been trying to kill off TRLA since what seems like the dawn of time.

In this episode, Senator Phil Gramm, Senator Kay Bailey Hutchison, Governor George W. Bush, Texas Secretary of State Tony Garza, and Tom Pauken are all calling for TRLA's collective head. And just what might this remarkably variegated cast of characters have in common? Do we notice a certain Republicaneity?

And just what has TRLA done this time to give Texas Republicans the hot fantods? Filed a perfectly good lawsuit, of course—so good that they've already won it.

Come with me now to the Rio Grande Valley, land of magical realism, where strange things are always happening. Down in Val Verde County, what to our wondering eyes should appear after the last election but an Anglo Republican sheriff and an Anglo Republican county commissioner—which seems unlikely, given that we're talking about Del Rio.

So the local Dems investigated and found that the R's' winning margins came from eight hundred votes mailed in by U.S. service personnel from around the world, most of whom had at some time or another been posted to Laughlin Air Force Base. Better than 90 percent of those votes went to the Republican candidates in the local elections. The problem is that under state and federal law, military personnel living abroad can vote only in federal elections. Many of the service folks voting in the Val Verde County commissioner's race have not lived in Del Rio in ten or even twenty years and know nothing about local issues or pols, so we see the wisdom of this restriction.

In truth, the reason that most of them continue to claim Del Rio and other Lone Star locales as a stateside residence is because Texas is one of seven states in our great nation that do not have a state income tax. In fact, military authorities regularly remind voting soldiers of this interesting fact, with the result that Texas, Florida, and Wyoming are the happy recipients of an exceptionally large chunk of the military vote. In Texas, depending on whom you talk to, we get between 50,000 and 200,000 votes from servicepeople who have not seen our shores in many, many moons.

None of this would be a problem if those in uniform got ballots listing only federal offices. Or even if the 254 county clerks in our state were all razor-sharp and knew election law cold. Not to cast aspersions on our very fine county clerks, but let's face it: Half of them are under average, which is how all those votes got counted in the Val Verde County commissioner's race.

And what a candidate was there elected by 113 votes. According to Germany's *Stern* magazine, commissioner-elect Murry Kachel, when he was stationed in that country about eight years ago, was active in the Ku Klux Klan. In fact, *Stern* ran a picture of him wearing his Klan robes accompanying a story reporting that he had been passed over for promotion precisely because of his KKK affiliation. Kachel denies the whole thing and says that *Stern* faked the picture and that he has never worn KKK robes or Bruno Magli shoes. The reporter who wrote the story is now a top editor at *Stern* and insists that the story and the picture are totally legit.*

So now we have Gramm, Hutchison, Bush, Pauken & Co. screaming that not only TRLA but the entire Legal Services Corporation should be defunded for casting aspersions on this splendid gentleman. The poor Legal Services Corporation, TRLA's bureaucratic parent, is under such heavy fire from the Republicans in Congress that it begged TRLA to drop the case, which was filed by TRLA attorney George Korbel.

So after Korbel got a temporary restraining order from U.S. District Judge H. F. "Hippo" Garcia, he lateraled the legal ball, as it were, to veteran Texas freedom-fighter David Richards, now in private practice. Richards in turn had little trouble persuading District Judge Fred Biery to enjoin the certification of the election of the two Val Verde Republicans.

All the Republican honchos have issued huffy statements saying that military personnel serving overseas should have the right to vote—as indeed they should, and not a soul has questioned it. But that doesn't have anything to do with the price of beans in Val Verde County.

Meanwhile, poor old TRLA is back on the railroad tracks again, with both its entire $3.4 million federal grant in jeopardy and also a chance to convince the state Legislature to help out with the cost of its noncontroversial services apparently in jeopardy.

Unlike California Legal Services, which apparently does harbor actual leftists (they have actual leftists in this state), TRLA consists of a bunch of bona fide, certified, chicken-fried good ol' Texas boys who happened to go to law school. That's probably where they picked up the foreign notion that even poor Hispanics have rights under the law, even in Texas.

Fort Worth Star-Telegram
January 26, 1997

---

* Kachel has since admitted the accuracy of *Stern*'s report.

Lone Star Republic

Called upon once more in my capacity as the World's Leading Authority on blue-bellied, wall-eyed, lithium-deprived Texas lunatics, I step modestly but confidently into the breach.

Yes, friends, I can explain why almost a dozen mush-brained lintheads holed up in the Davis Mountains demanding that Texas become a free country once again. I cannot explain why the national media chose to describe these oxygen-deprived citizens as "Texas separatists"—as though being a Texas separatist were something within the realm of loosely circumscribed sanity—but then, not even Slats Grobnik could explain everything.

The self-proclaimed "Republic of Texas" is a set of folks descended from the Texas property-rights movement. The property-rights movement, known further west as the Wise Use movement, surfaced here in the summer of 1994, born in a state of high indignation and profound misunderstanding.

The folks in property rights were upset over the prospect that the gummint might take their property without giving them any recompense. These folks were not reassured by the very words in the Constitution that say the gummint cannot take your property without giving you fair value for it. During one memorable exchange on this point, Marshall Kuykendall, president of the group Take Back Texas, replied to some legalistic quibbler who asked for a specific case of gummint taking property: "When Lincoln freed the slaves, he did not pay for them."

You have to admit, ol' Marshall has you there.

Now, while that story is quite true, in fairness, it makes the property-rights folks look a lot dumber than they actually are. It is widely understood and accepted, even in Texas, that you cannot do whateverthehell you damn please with your own property if it will have a seriously adverse effect on your neighbors. You cannot be building some plant with a lot of toxic emissions if it will cause the neighbors to die, for example. Reasonable people can agree on that.

But in central Texas, the slightly more communistic area of the state, environmentalists have successfully filed a bunch of lawsuits, leaving the courts pondering how much property has to be set aside to maintain a habitat for two endangered species: the black-capped vireo, a pretty songbird, and the Barton Creek salamander, a critter only a herpetologist could love.

Envision this from the property owner's point of view: Here you are settin' on several acres of increasingly valuable land on the edge of these boomin' cities—either Austin or San Antone. You got these high-tech companies—IBM, Texas Instruments, whoever—just beggin' you to let 'em build a nice, new plant on your place. And some fool is goin' to screw this up over a salamander? And while this salamander deal is bein' decided, is anybody goin' to pay you for the money you're losin'?

So there you have the nub of your property-rights movement, which also involves more generalized antienvironmentalist sentiment, plus a lot of fed-cussing.

So how'd we get from fair questions to *las cucarachas* in the Davis Mountains? Easy. The property-rights movement always did shade gradually from folks who sound just like every grump you've ever heard grousin' about the goddamn gummint to total fruitcakes. The fruitcake end of the spectrum naturally shaded into the militia movement. As Jim Hamblin of San Marcos, a member of the Texas Constitutional Militia, once inquired reasonably, "Why are they so afraid of a few hundred thousand people with assault rifles?"

But out there on the far end of the militia movement—mostly a bunch of guys who like to play soldier—you find your folks into *The Turner Diaries,* race war, and bombing federal buildings. Slippery slopes.

The Republic of Texas in turn has two branches: the nearly normal lunatics who claim to be the official Republic of Texas and the Richard Lance, McLaren branch. McLaren has been filing phony liens since 1985 and is splendidly obsessive: He has written thousands and thousands of pages of legal documents, briefs, appeals, warrants, liens, proclamations—a sort of vast parody of the law.

Two things worth noting about the ROT folks. One is, you listen to these guys long enough and they will start to remind you of the kids who used to get so heavily involved in the game Dungeons and Dragons that they lost track of reality. At some point, imagination becomes delusion. And this group delusion is spread through the Internet.

One cannot blame computers for this, since history is full of examples of not just the *folie à deux* but the *folie à large numbers.* But computers do facilitate the phenomenon.

The second important point about ROT and its followers is that they should not be dismissed with the old put-down "Get a life." That's the problem. They can't. Most of them don't have the education or the skills to get and keep a decent job. They're going to spend the rest of their lives in trailer parks. Basically, these guys are Bubba. A little stranger than Bubba usually is, but still Bubba. Maybe a high school education. Twenty, make that almost thirty, years of falling wages. No way to get ahead. And all day they listen to the establishment media tell them the economy is booming. Everyone else is getting rich. Mansions are selling like hotcakes. Big cigars and thick steaks are fashionable again. The angst of the soccer mom is the highest concern of our politicians.

There is so much anger out here. It is taking so many bizarre forms. And most of the media can't even see it: economic apartheid keeps the bottom half of this society well hidden from the top half. Texas Attorney General Dan Morales says ROT is "terrorism, pure and simple."

We all feel real bad about the one fella who was killed in the deal: we thought we'd gotten out of it without bloodshed, but two of 'em took to the hills. The official explanation is that Mike Matson, forty-eight, was shot by a Texas Department of Criminal Justice dog handler after he had fired on a state helicopter. But it should be noted that Matson had shot three dogs at that point.

"Dingbattery, pure and simple" I could buy. Terrorism? Because a lot of Americans cannot forgive what happened at Waco and Ruby Ridge? Why should they? Ever heard anyone apologize for those murders? A lot of Americans have no hope, get no help, and see their own government as an oppressive force. For them, it is, isn't it? Working-class people are getting screwed by their own government. Its latest start is to cut the capital-gains tax and the estate tax that kicks in after a person leaves more than $600,000. More tax breaks for the rich mean a larger share of the tax burden for everybody else.

What we have here is just a little case of misdirected anger. O.K., the U.N. and black helicopters are not the problem. But don't underestimate the anger itself.

The Nation
May 26, 1997

Sic Transit Gloria Annie

Ave atque vale, Governor Richards. *Adios,* Annie. Keep your wagon between the ditches. May your days be full of laughter. Good on ya.

Ann Richards's electoral loss to George Dubya Bush will keep political scientists studying for years. By all the conventional measures, she should have walked back into office. Her approval rating was and is over 60 percent—practically golden. The state's economy is ginnin', crime rates are down, school scores are up, she never raised taxes, never had a scandal.

The short, easy version is that Richards lost because of President Clinton. In Florida, where Clinton was at 42 percent in the approval ratings, Governor Lawton Chiles pulled it out. In Texas, where Clinton hovers around 36 percent, there just wasn't a shot. Another short, easy version is that she won by 100,000 votes last time against a gloriously inept opponent, and in the meantime, 120,000 people have moved into the state and registered Republican.

The more complex and more accurate version is that George Dubya ran a helluva campaign and Annie ran a dud. Their race became a peculiar black-and-white negative of the 1992 presidential race between George Dubya's daddy and Clinton, with Richards as the stay-the-course, no-vision candidate and Bush as the proponent of change, change, change. George Dubya's campaign was full of ideas and plans (of dubious merit, but what the hey), while Richards neither successfully sold what should have been limned as a brilliant record nor projected any enthusiasm for a wonderful future. The New Texas disappeared. The television ads were lousy.

A lot of they-sayers believe Richards & Co. underestimated George Dubya, who ain't no Claytie Williams. I thought she took him seriously from the git-go, which is why she flip-flopped on federal protection for Caddo Lake, thus royally annoying the enviros. But dismissing him as a "jerk" set off the now famous angry-white-male vote. I'm not sure what Richards could have done to win over that vote; my personal opinion is that some men feel threatened by a strong woman, especially one with a quick tongue.

In addition, there was the God, gays, and guns factor. As always, there was a campaign that ran below the radar, particularly in East Texas. Richards staffers dreamed up a game: Put a certain bumper sticker on your car and drive through East Texas, and whoever got back to Waco alive would be the winner. The bumper sticker would read, I'M THE QUEER ANN SENT HERE TO TAKE YOUR GUNS AWAY.

Of the hundreds of distinguished appointments that Richards made, which will surely include the black, brown, and female leaders of the coming years, only a literal handful were gays or lesbians. But the Christian right, using the fear-mongering hyperbole for which it is so noted, managed to imply that the capital had become a sink of iniquity. Richards's veto of the concealed-weapons bill set off the gun nuts. I still think it was statesmanship of a high order.

As for Richards's real record in office, to the extent that the governor of Texas is really nothing more than a salesman for the state, I'm not sure we've ever had a better. Richards is as popular outside Texas as she is inside. And although her sense of humor may have cost her votes with the angry white males, I think she has definitely proved again that it is possible to hold high public office and be witty, too.

Her biggest mistake in my book was early on, when Bob Bullock had the guts to come out for a state income tax and Richards left him out there slowly twisting in the wind. (So did the bidness community, which has quietly been in favor of same for many years.) That was gutless.

In the bidness community's books, Richards's appointments in insurance, environment, and nursing-home regulation were "too militant." Bidness people felt they were perceived as the enemy when they went in to deal with those folks, and no one likes that. There's an extent to which it was a real problem with some of Richards's more purist appointments, and an extent to which it was nothing more than willful misperception. Besides, anyone who doesn't make enemies in office isn't worth spit.

Richards said in a farewell interview with the press corps that if she'd known she was going to be a one-term governor, she would have "raised more hell." I wish she had. But these are relatively minor quibbles with what is, overall, a distinguished record. My political memory of Texas governors goes back to Allan Shivers, and I know that in that time we have not had a governor who worked nearly as hard as Ann Richards. Who was nearly as gracious as Richards. Who made more good appointments than Richards. Who set a higher standard of honesty than Richards.

A special thanks is due Richards from recovering alcoholics and addicts all over the country. Her grassroots work in this field, done in addition to her duties as governor, has been tireless, inspirational, and quite simply extraordinary. From mansions in Dallas to prisons all over the state, she has changed lives. To see the governor of Texas sitting in a circle with convicted convicts saying simply, "My name is Ann and I am an alcoholic" is to learn a great deal about recovery.

What our notoriously weak governors actually do is set a tone for the state. So let it be recorded that for four brief shining years, Ann Richards gave the joint some class.

Good on ya, Annie. So now go camping and have some fun.

Fort Worth Star-Telegram
January 8, 1995

The National
Politician of Texas

For years now, whenever there's been a gathering of Bullockians—
those who study Texas's most amazing living politician—the scholars
always end by asking the same question: "Who's gonna write the
book?"

Someone has to. Not since Lyndon Johnson has there been another
pol who could so dominate everyone around him by sheer force of personality. Bob Bullock is probably the smartest person I've ever known,
which is partly what makes both the good and the bad of him so outsize. As George Reedy once said of LBJ, "He may have been a son of a
bitch, but he was a colossal son of a bitch."

We won't lose Bullock until January 1999, but we are damn sure
losin' a tall tree here. He's almost sixty-eight, has had part of one lung
removed and bypass surgery, did untold damage to himself with alcohol, is slightly deaf, is manic-depressive, and still works harder, thinks
faster, and knows more than anyone else in Texas government. And
maybe in Texas.

Some facts about the lieutenant governor:

• He sleeps about four hours a night. His staffers are all accustomed to the 2:00 A.M. phone call: "What about this? Did we get that done? Let's try it another way." His most notable personal characteristic is loyalty: If you're a friend of Bullock's, you're a friend of Bullock's no matter what you do or what happens to you—if you wind up in prison or in the gutter, he'll still be there for you. The one thing he cannot tolerate is disloyalty.

• Bad-tempered? You haven't really worked for Bullock unless he's fired you at least once. If you're any good, he unfires you right away.

• He has the greatest wicked chuckle you have ever heard.

• He comes to his office every morning at 6:30 A.M. and spends an hour working on the twelve steps of Alcoholics Anonymous.

• Abner McCall gave him a D in ethics at Baylor Law School.

• Best thing that ever happened to Bullock: In 1985, Jan Teague, showing great courage but only arguable good sense, agreed to become his fifth wife. (Actually, Bullock remarried his first wife, Amelia, the mother of his children, after his second marriage, so there have been only three of them, if you don't count the annulment, but it's a little complicated to explain.)

• Brains and hard work are only two of the sources of Bullock's power—the other is that he's a bad man to cross. You don't want this man as an enemy, because he will get you, he will pay you back. He's far more mellow these days than he used to be, but there was a time when Bullock could be meaner than a skilletful of rattlesnakes.

Heart attacks, grand juries, DWI's, divorces—this isn't a story, it's a saga. Of course there is a difference between Bullock in his drinking days and Bullock today—he's not quite a different person, but he sure is easier. He went off to "Whiskey School" in California in 1981. Six weeks later he returned to Austin in the middle of the night, sober and alone. Only one person came out to the airport to meet him— Ann Richards. He has never forgotten that kindness.

Just a couple of stories from the drinking years: One night Bullock and his pal Nick Kralj (Bullock used to have any number of reprehensible friends) got took bad drunk, went into the basement of Kralj's nightclub, and proceeded to shoot roaches with pistols. They claimed it took great skill.

On another occasion, one of Bullock's early wives kicked him out of the house, presumably for good cause. So he went to crash with his friend Carlton Carl, who was himself out drinking. Unable to get into Carl's apartment, Bullock crawled into the backseat of Carl's car, which was parked in an alley, got under a blanket, and passed out there. Unfortunately, it wasn't Carl's car, just looked like it. When Bullock came to the next morning, he was being driven along I-35 by a total stranger who had no idea anyone was in the backseat. After pondering his options, Bullock sat up and said to the unsuspecting citizen, "Hi there, I'm Bob Bullock, your secretary of state." Poor guy almost drove off the road.

Bullock as a public official: Only twice in thirty years as a political reporter have I seen an official completely remake a government bureaucracy. Ann Richards did it at the treasurer's office by slowly winning the trust and confidence of the employees. Bob Bullock did it at the comptroller's office by kicking ass until hell wouldn't have it. He terrified those poor state bureaucrats. Fired a lot of them too.

Under Bullock's relentless, driving energy, the comptroller's office started collecting taxes that had been allowed to slide for years. You paid your nickel to Bullock, or he'd come down on you like a gullywasher. He was such a tax-collectin' sumbitch that the Lege used to give his office more money every year so he could go out and collect more, and they wouldn't have to raise taxes. That worked for over ten years. I once ran across an Arizona official who assured me, in the reverent tones normally reserved for the Lord, "Bob Bullock is a *legend* in comptrolling circles." I assured her he was legend in many others as well.

When Bullock became comptroller in 1975, he inherited several thousand employees, but not one of them above the level of janitor was black. Bullock was determined to change that. He soon learned he couldn't attract the top black graduates of the UT law school with a state salary. So he went around to every little black college he could find and personally took out the professors in accounting, computers, management—all the skills he needed at his shop—and convinced them to send him the names of their top five graduates every year. The state has gotten some incredibly fine employees through this method. Now, that's affirmative action.

After sixteen years as comptroller, Bullock understood the state's tax system—both where the money comes from and how it's spent—better than anyone alive. You add that knowledge to the power that comes from his current office—under the constitution and the senate rules, the lite guv has more power than anyone else in state government—and you've got the juggernaut that is Bullock.

As far as I know, Bullock has no ideology. He is a pragmatist, a problem-solver, and a deal-maker. Although no one would call him scholarly, Bullock studies public policy all the time. He reads, he picks people's brains; he is hungry, he is avid for information. He also uses it for political advantage.

His Texas patriotism is famous, and there is nothing phony or political about it. He ends every speech with "God bless Texas" and means it. When Bullock returned from the Korean War in the fifties, he got down on his knees, kissed the soil of Texas, and swore never to leave it again, a vow he kept for about twenty-five years, until curiosity drew him to Mexico. Jan has made him into something of a traveler.

Bullock is one of the greatest natural Texas speakers I have ever known. He uses the inherited sayings frequently, "lookin' wise as a treeful of owls," "slicker 'n bus-station chili." But he also invents his own metaphors and similes, most of them unprintable. He was once trying to describe a city slicker of a reporter to whom he had taken a dislike, and said, "His pants was so tight, if he'd a' farted, it woulda' blowed his boots off." Bullock off the record is politically incorrect about seventy dozen times a day.

Bullock is what feminists sometimes refer to sarcastically as "a manly man." (Bullock calls feminists "them hairy-legged wimmin," but he has a damn good record on women's issues.) The drinking, the fighting, the hunting, the cussing, the woman troubles—if this guy was starting out in politics today, he couldn't get elected weigher of hides. What we now call "the character issue" would keep him out of office. But think of the loss that would be to this state. When you compare Bob Bullock to today's crop of blow-dried, priggish, goody-two-shoe, suburban bores, it's enough to make you homesick for the old Texas.

But I think the real difference between Bullock and a lot of pols today is much more than style. This is a man who has sought power and *knows what he wants to use it for.* Look at the poll-driven pols, scratching around for a popular issue they can ride to higher office. Bullock has always known what he wanted to do: get power, use it to help people (and screw some enemies)—especially people who don't get dealt much of a hand to start with—and to make the state a better place. God bless Texas.

Fort Worth Star-Telegram
June 8, 1997

Tributes to
Souls Passing

The Death of
a Beauty Queen

MELBOURNE, AUSTRALIA — They just called from Texas to tell me that Sammilu Williamson Evans, who was Miss Texas in 1960-something (Samm would not appreciate having her age so much as implied) committed suicide yesterday. God rest you, Samm, God rest you.

I would like for you to have the pleasure of knowing her a little, not so much Samm as she was but Samm as she would have liked you to think of her, Samm as she worked so hard to be—bright and golden and funny. She was a work of art, that Samm, the absolute apogee (that means The Top, Samm) of a certain kind of Texas woman. She was like the prettiest Christmas package you ever saw, so sparkly and charming. And inside were the gifts she never gave herself credit for— warmth and honesty and guts and humor.

Samm Evans was either ridiculously pretty or actually beautiful, I'm not sure which, but I wish that I, or anyone else, had been able to convince her that her looks were the least part of her being a knockout. God knows, she worked at it. Her hair was big and blond and poofy; the nails, perfect; the makeup, flawless; her clothes were smashingly sexy; and her figure, believe me, could still stop traffic at the age of mmmm-something. She was, she often said, a high-maintenance kind of woman.

But Samm was a lot more than surface. I liked her humor most—it was sassy and self-mocking. Once when she was slightly overdoing her ditzy-blonde routine, I teased her, saying, "C'mon, Samm, quit trying for Miss Congeniality."

Sammilu Williamson Evans, veteran of a zillion beauty contests, drew herself up in great dignity and with her unmistakable Texas accent said, "My motto was always *death* before Miss Congeniality."

But even more important than her humor was her warmth: Samm loved to do things for other people. But she was not good at letting other people do things for her; she worked too hard at being perfect.

Samm was such a fitness buff that at one point George Bush was going to name her to the President's Council on Physical Fitness. Samm would have adored hanging out with Arnold Schwarzenegger—she did enjoy knowing celebrities. But instead she wound up at the Betty Ford Center at the beginning of a long struggle against the disease that finally killed her. She was the first to point out the delicious irony of winding up at Betty Ford instead of on the Council for Physical Fitness.

As for why Samm and I became friends, it was really quite simple: I appreciated her art form. I know how much work it takes to look that good all the time. And I liked her honesty. Samm had no side. She was part of what I think of as Houston café society, and she cared desperately about a lot of things I don't give a damn about. But she never pretended to be anything other than a kid who came from the Heights, back when it was a tacky, lower-middle-class neighborhood. She went to Reagan High and "attended," as they say, the University of Houston, where she sure as hell never got asked to join a fancy sorority.

If anyone inquired about the name Samm, she would hoot with glee about the absurdity of having been stuck with a Texas-tacky monicker like "Sammilu." She adored her second husband, Ken Evans, to whom she was married for eight years, and wanted so desperately to be part of his world that she would talk about "our grandchildren." Losing a stepdaughter to cancer earlier this year, compounded by the death of her own mother this summer, sent her into a state of high brittleness. Everything was fine, everything was lovely, she was recovering well, she needed no help.

Her long-dead father was an alcoholic, and who knows how much Mama Rose there was in Samm's mother? The first beauty title she ever won was Baby Miss Houston at age three months.

So if Samm Evans was so beautiful and charming and married to this wonderful guy and materialistic enough to love having diamonds and jetting to favorite restaurants and having the little red convertible with SAMM on the vanity plates, how come she took a dive off a twenty-third-story balcony in the Galleria area in November?

She had a fatal illness. When Samm was trying to recover from alcoholism, it took her a long time to figure out that it doesn't make any difference whether you get drunk on Stoli in a twenty-third-story penthouse or drunk on Thunderbird in the gutter—it's the same disease. She died with a blood-alcohol level of 0.50.

We were the unlikeliest friends, given our personalities, but I got a note from her a few months ago. It says, "Thank you for taking me seriously."

Fort Worth Star-Telegram
December 12, 1993

Remembering Dick

Quel triumph for the old Trickster. One last time we got a new Nixon. The Dead Nixon was, according to all those glowing tributes on television, a man of vision, courage, and leadership. For those of you thinking you must have lost your marbles lately to have forgotten what a great American Richard Nixon was, here's a little pop quiz to refresh your memories.

•*How did Bob Haldeman, who was Nixon's closest aide in the White House, describe Nixon in writing from prison?*
"Dirty, mean, coldly calculating, devious, craftily manipulative, the weirdest man ever to live in the White House."

•*What did Nixon think of the Supreme Court?*
He nominated two men, Clement Haynsworth and G. Harrold Carswell, to the Court, both of whom were found unfit to serve there by the United States Senate. According to Haldeman, if Nixon had gotten a single vote on the Court, he would have defied its order to turn

over the Watergate tapes. "When the Court ruled 8-to-0 against Nixon, it unknowingly averted what might have been a supremely critical confrontation between the executive and judiciary powers."

•*How did Nixon see the executive branch?*

According to John Ehrlichman, shortly before the 1972 election Nixon called a "landmark meeting" at Camp David to plan the "capture" of the executive branch. "It was Nixon's intent to repopulate the bureaucracy with our people. We would seek new laws to permit the dead and disloyal wood to be cast out." Nixon admired John Dean because "he had the kind of steel and really mean instinct we needed to clean house after the election in various departments and to put the IRS and Justice Department on the kind of basis it should be on." The IRS was to be used to get those on the enemies list.

In his diary Nixon wrote, "There simply has to be a line drawn at times with those who are against us, and then we have to take action to deal with them effectively." Of a bureaucrat who had failed to knuckle under to the White House, Nixon said, "We're going to get him . . . there are many unpleasant places a bureaucrat can be sent." At other times, Nixon ranted about the "Jewish cabal" in the bureaucracy he was convinced was trying to make him look bad and ordered a head count of Jews in certain sections of the government.

"The Democrats have the Jews and the Negroes, and let them have them. In fact, tie them around their necks," Nixon said. He hated the "Jewish press" (i.e., the major newspapers) and warned an aide to "stay away from the arts—the arts are full of Jews." He used the word *nigger* and believed blacks were genetically inferior.

•*What did Nixon think of reformers?*

Hated them. Those who harped on honesty in government were "hypocrites, little bastards, sanctimonious frauds, people who couldn't butter a piece of bread."

•*And what did Nixon think of the American people?*
He told Theodore White about campaigning. "All the while you're smiling, you want to kick them in the shins."

•*How many Americans died in Vietnam after Richard Nixon ran on a platform of having a "secret plan" to end the war and promised to get us out within six months of his inauguration?*
Twenty-one thousand.

•*What was the Huston Plan, and who felt it threatened civil liberties?*
The Huston Plan was intended to control Nixon's enemies by wire-tapping their phones, opening their mail, burglarizing their homes and offices. J. Edgar Hoover was horrified by it. It was the official policy of the administration and suspended the Fourth Amendment.

•*How did historian Barbara Tuchman describe Nixon's legacy?*
"An accumulated tale of cover-up, blackmail, suborned testimony, hush money, espionage, sabotage, use of federal powers for the harassment of 'enemies,' and a program by some fifty hired operators to pervert and subvert the campaigns of Democratic candidates by 'dirty tricks,' or what in the choice language of the White House crew was referred to as 'ratfucking.' The final list of indictable crimes would include burglary, bribery, forgery, perjury, theft, conspiracy, and obstructing justice."

•*How did Charles Colson describe George McGovern's 1972 campaign?*
"Just about the dirtiest, meanest presidential campaign in this nation's history."

•*Richard Nixon has been described by his biographer as "a humorless man"; did he ever say anything funny?*
Yes. Upon being shown the Great Wall of China, Nixon said, "This is, indeed, a great wall."

The Progressive
June 1994

The Person Who Kept the
Texas Observer Running

Clifford Richard Olafson, sixty-four, who served as business manager of the *Texas Observer* magazine for thirty years, died Saturday of lung cancer. He was the most Christ-like person I have ever known.

Clif grew up in a tough, working-class, ethnic neighborhood in Minneapolis. His mom died when he was twelve, and I had the impression that his dad was a bit of a hard-horse—at any rate, there was a gulf between them. Clif left home right out of high school and joined the Navy. He sailed the world for seven years, and his only un-seamanlike trait was that he never told stories about that time.

He left the Navy in search of a higher purpose and wound up joining the old Christian Faith and Life community in Texas, a cooperative of gentle souls dedicated to living out Christian principles in daily practice by serving others. Sarah Payne, the *Observer*'s first business manager and a love of a woman, found Clif for us there. She persuaded him that organizing and managing the business (or unglamorous) side of a tiny, liberal magazine devoted to trying to make Texas a better place was the right role for him. Never has an enterprise been so lucky.

I always thought of Clif as a man's man, although I suppose that's ironic, since he was gay. He came from a time and a place where being homosexual was deeply shameful, so one had to know him for many years before it was ever mentioned. So many of his virtues were masculine; he was like an Owen Wister hero or a Gary Cooper cowboy character. He was terribly shy, so he seldom had much to say. He never fussed or complained; he just got things done.

He could fix anything—often with nothing more than a screwdriver and a roll of duct tape—from a malfunctioning electric coffeepot to a cranky addressing machine. We used to say: "He carps! He plumbs! He paints! He electrics!" He was a walking, one-man craft union. If Clif couldn't build it himself, he'd go buy whatever we needed from a junkyard and fix that. He was a specialist in the naval art of jury-rigging whatever was needed. Who among the regular visitors to the old *Observer* office will forget the screwdriver-through-the-hasp that served as the handle on the ancient refrigerator that Clif had resurrected, and painted sky-blue, to store our precious supply of Lone Star beer?

Like most sailors, Clif could neatly stow away an amazing amount of stuff in a very small space, shipshape and Bristol-fashion. His business practices, while as meticulous as all his work, also involved some jury-rigging. He took accounting and other business courses; he did the books, fund-raising, mailing, advertising, billing, expenses, taxes, you name it. We were always skating on the thin edge of being broke, so Clif kept three accounts for the *Observer*, and in the days before computers put the kibosh on it, he could keep us going for days on "float," moving money from one account to another.

When times were dire, Clif simply did not draw his salary. We were all paid poverty wages; only Clif—and Kaye Northcott, who has no vices—ever saved money on an *Observer* salary: it turns out that Clif saved $10,000 during thirty-two years of working for the *Observer*. He has left it all to the *Observer*.

Clif did not care about worldly goods, so he had only thrifty and practical possessions. I once asked him to help me set up an office at home; Clif built me a desk out of concrete blocks and an old door he had been keeping handy, a lamp (fixed it himself, of course), a chair (perfectly good, from Goodwill), and a typewriter (bought as junk, repaired by Clif). The total cost was $7.

Clif worked days, nights, and weekends; he could always find something that needed doing. Whenever there was something to be done, Clif would pitch in and do it—no fuss, no complaint, just the flash of that shy grin and "Here, let me help." If our neighbors needed heavy objects hoisted up the stairs, Clif would do it. If, in the vast circle of *Observer* friends and family, someone needed help moving, cleaning out the garage, changing the oil in the car, getting a keg to a party, whatever, Clif would do it. The number of old clunker cars he kept rolling for us all would have done a large garage proud.

I have occasionally run into people around central Texas—thrifty, hardworking, practical people who run hardware stores, machine shops, junk stores—who know Clif and shake their heads in admiration. "That Clif Olafson, now he's a good fella. That's a smart fella." Perhaps they would have been repulsed if they had known that Clif was gay. But I rather doubt it. Clif was just so . . . good. And competent.

In his "spare time," Clif acted as a mentor to a series of hard-luck Chicano teen-agers, teaching them reading and writing and then accounting or a manual skill, so they could get good jobs. Years later, when one of his protégés, Joe Espinoza of the million-dollar smile, was dying of AIDS, Clif nursed him tenderly to his last day. Another one of Clif's kids, Juan, came back up from Mexico to nurse Clif at the end.

Like many people who grow up poor, Clif had bad teeth, broken and uneven, although he got them fixed late in his life. And like most people with bad teeth, Clif seldom smiled, or at least covered his mouth when he did so. But every now and again, when you really managed to amuse him with some outrageous tale of Texas politics, he would throw back his head and laugh, and it was just like sunshine.

He was a decent, gentle, honorable man. I would close by wishing a pox on all who would think ill of him because he was gay. But Clif would never have done that; he would only have said, "Here, let me help."

Clif and I talked about beer, sports, cars, dogs—what I consider "guy stuff." He had other friends with whom he discussed his long, tireless search for spiritual improvement.

I never saw a trace of religiosity in him. Where did it come from, all that love and generosity, all that goodness and giving? God only knows. And that is the answer, of course.

Fort Worth Star-Telegram
December 19, 1995

She Sounded Like God

Finding Barbara Jordan in the directory of distinguished Americans is easy. She was always a First and an Only.

First woman, only black; in the Texas Senate, in the Texas congressional delegation, from the entire South. She served on the Judiciary Committee during the decision on Richard Nixon's impeachment. Her great bass voice rolled forth: "My faith in the Con-sti-tu-tion is whole, it is com-plete, it is to-tal." She sounded like the Lord God Almighty, and her implacable legal logic caught the attention of the entire nation.

The degree of prejudice she had to overcome by intelligence and sheer force of personality is impossible to overestimate. She wasn't just black and female: She was homely, she was heavy, and she was dark black. When she first came to the Texas Senate, one of her colleagues referred to her as "that nigger mammy washerwoman." It was considered a great joke to bring racist friends to the gallery when B.J. was due to speak. They would no sooner gasp, "Who is that nigger?" than she would open her mouth and out would roll language Lincoln would have appreciated. Her personal dignity was so substantial even admirers hesitated to approach her. No one will ever know how lonely she was at the beginning.

Her friend Representative Eleanor Holmes Norton justly reminds us that B.J. was not effective solely because she sounded like God. Born and raised in the Fifth Ward of Houston, the biggest black ghetto in the biggest state, she graduated magna cum laude from Texas Southern University and went on to Boston University Law School. Jordan was so smart it almost hurt. Lord, she was a good legislator, never wasted a minute on a hopeless cause. Ask those cornered-cottonmouth, mean-as-hell-with-the-hide-off conservatives. Fought her on the floor in head-up debate, fought her in the back room over Article 53, Subsection C, Part II: Jordan always knew what she was talking about and almost always won. She traded some public suck-up with the Texas Democratic establishment—Lyndon Johnson, Ben Barnes—and got the first black congressional district drawn in Texas. Smart trade.

As it happened, the night B.J. spoke to Congress in favor of impeaching Richard Nixon was also the last night of the Texas legislative session. Came B.J.'s turn to speak and everyone back in Austin—legislators, aides, janitors, maids—gathered around television sets to hear this black woman speak on national television. And they cheered for her as though they were watching the University of Texas pound hell out of Notre Dame in the Cotton Bowl.

She cut her congressional career short; it seems likely that she knew she had multiple sclerosis. Of course, she wanted a seat on the Supreme Court. If there is one thing I would ask you to accept on faith, it is that Barbara Jordan had Judicial Temperament. Her faith in the Con-sti-tu-tion was whole, it was complete, it was total. I consulted her about appointments from Robert Bork to Clarence Thomas and never found her less than fair. George Bush the Elder will tell you the same.

In the last fourteen years of her life, B.J. was a magnificent teacher, at the LBJ School of Public Affairs. The only way to get into her classes at the University of Texas was to win a place in a lottery. For many students, she was the inspiration for a life in public service. No perks, no frills, no self-righteousness: just a solid commitment to using government to help achieve liberty and justice for all. Her role as a role model may well have been her most important. One little black girl used to walk by Jordan's house every day on her way to school and think, "Barbara Jordan grew up right here, too." Today Ruth Simmons is president of Smith College.

Jordan was a helluva poker player. And before M.S. twisted her poor hands so badly, she loved to play guitar. It was like God singing the blues. "St. James Infirmary"—Let her go, *Looord,* let her go.

But let's not let her go without remembering that the Woman Who Sounded Like God had a very dry sense of humor. One time, she invited Ann Richards, then a mere county commissioner, over for dinner. Jordan lived down a dirt road and had a troublesome neighbor who kept locking the gates on it. Jordan, never one to miss an opportunity to Make Government Work, asked the commissioner to do something. Richards made some phone calls, to no avail.

Time went by, and Jordan again invited Richards, by then governor of Texas, to dinner. Richards inquired idly: "Barbara, whatever happened to that dreadful neighbor of yours? Did she ever quit lockin' the gates?"

Jordan said: "I am pleased to report that the woman in question has since died. And gone to hell."

Today Barbara Jordan is the first and only black woman resting in the Texas State Cemetery.

The New York Times Magazine
December 29, 1996

Queen of the Muckrakers

Jessica Mitford Romilly Treuhaft, known as Decca, who died last month, was among the handful of great muckraking journalists of our time. Peter Sussman of the Society of Professional Journalists puts her in a class with Upton Sinclair, Rachel Carson, and Ralph Nader. "Only funny."

Always funny. Lord knows, she could bring 'em down. She drove the entire funeral industry into collective apoplexy with *The American Way of Death* (1963), eventually leading the Federal Trade Commission to issue regulations for the industry; drove the Famous Writers School into richly deserved bankruptcy; and, in general, had quite a string of notches on her gun. She was also a wit, a charmer, a rebel, an ex-Communist, a lifelong radical, a beauty, and a lady. She led the most extraordinary life, with honor and with humor throughout.

Think of the leftist women writers of her generation and ask yourself who you would have wanted to be friends with. Lillian Hellman, with all that Sturm und Drang? Mary McCarthy, with that backstabbing streak? Nonsense. You would have wanted to know Decca, of course, because she was such fun.

Toward the end of her life she was working on an update of *The American Way of Death,* for which reason she arrived in Houston last summer to visit the American Funeral Museum, of which it must be said, it's there. It's a multimedia museum. We toddled through the exhibits until we reached Embalming, where we perched on a bench to view a short documentary. Pyramids appeared on screen, and the narrator announced portentously, "The art of embalming was first discovered by the ancient Egyptians."

Decca said quietly, "Now *there* was a culture where the funeral directors got *completely* out of control."

She was hot on the trail of the story of the astonishing new concentration of ownership in the funeral industry. Except it's now called "the death-services industry," with that penchant for ghastly euphemism Decca pilloried so memorably. Something called Service Corporation International is swallowing its competition at such a clip that before long we'll all have to pay them to get planted. Decca went off incognito to price crypts at a local S.C.I. crematorium. The "grief counselor" started by showing her the el cheapo model. "Wouldn't be caught dead in it," she snorted.

The newsmagazines invariably used to start profiles of Decca, "Born the daughter of an eccentric British peer . . ." as though she had done nothing else in her life. But it was a lulu of a family. To take it at a gallop, her eldest sister was the splendid comic novelist Nancy Mitford; her sister Diana married Sir Oswald Mosley, a leading British fascist, and spent World War II in prison; her sister Unity fell in love with Hitler and shot herself at the outbreak of the war; her brother, Tom, was killed in Burma; her sister Pamela raised horses; and her sister Debo became the duchess of Devonshire.

Decca Mitford sensibly decided to get out of the nest at an early age: she eloped with her cousin Esmond Romilly when she was nineteen and went off to fight for the Communists in the Spanish Civil War. Since both were scions of great families, a British destroyer was dispatched to bring them back. They married in France, but not until later: *quel scandale.*

The Romillys immigrated to America in 1939, tended bar, sold stockings, what have you. All fodder for great stories later told by Decca. Romilly enlisted in the Royal Canadian Air Force ("I'll probably find myself being commanded by one of your ghastly relations," he observed) and was killed in action in 1941, leaving Decca with their baby daughter, Dinky. (So strong is the Mitford mania for nicknames that I never knew Dinky's real name was Constancia until I read it in Decca's obituary.) She went to work for the Office of Price Administration in Washington and moved in with those generous progressive Southern souls Clifford and Virginia Durr. Since Decca and Virginia both had the gift of making hardship into marvelous stories, tales of that household have become almost legendary.

In 1943 Decca married Robert Treuhaft, a calm, witty, radical, Harvard-trained lawyer. They were married for fifty-three years, and for fifty-three years she was in love with him. Thought he hung the moon, and all that other 1930s love-ballad stuff. Her dear friend Maya Angelou recalled, "My God, they had been married for *two hundred years* and every time she heard his car pull up in the driveway she'd say, 'Bob's here; it's Bob!' "

Decca once said that she felt she had never really known her sister Nancy because Nancy lived within an "armor of drollery." Decca herself would make almost anything into a joke: When summoned to appear before the House Un-American Activities Committee in San Francisco, she took the per diem expense check she got from the government and donated it to the Communist party. She and her husband remained party members in Oakland, California, until 1958; their adventures are described in her political memoir, *A Fine Old Conflict.*

A Decca story from the C.P. days: She had long since realized that fund-raisers and parties were part of "the struggle." Some humorless party apparatchik had entrusted her with organizing a chicken dinner for the faithful and was giving her instructions. When it came to procuring the main course, he wanted to direct Decca to politically correct poultry farmers. He looked left and looked right, apparently suspicious of FBI wiretaps. "There are certain comrades in—" he broke off. He scribbled a note and pushed it across his desk. "Petaluma," it read. After further instruction, Decca said she had just one question. "Do you think the chickens should be—" she began. She looked left, looked right, checking for bugs, and scribbled, "broiled or fried?"

A not-so-funny Decca story: At the height of the McCarthy era, that great liberal Hubert H. Humphrey proposed that membership in the Communist party be made a crime. Decca was trying to explain to Dinky, then eight, that all of them might be sent away to detention camp. "Camp?!" cried Dinky in delight, envisioning tennis and canoeing. Decca told it as a good story. Armored with drollery.

Decca Mitford was not fearless; she was brave. Much as she ridiculed those English public-school virtues, like spunk and pluck, she was herself guilty of one of them: She was gallant. Her gallantry was more than simple courage. It sometimes takes courage to see injustice and then stand up and denounce it. Gallantry requires doing so without ever becoming bitter; gallantry requires humor and honor.

Decca and her friend Marge Frantz invented the "roar-o-meter" to measure how absurd the world could be. Much as she relished the world's silliness, there is a true north in all her work—a passion for social justice and concern for those who are being beaten and battered.

I think some people who knew her only slightly assumed Decca Mitford glided through this world with the complete self-assurance that comes from an aristocratic background. She was not much given to regrets—I don't think anyone ever heard her whine about anything, even though she lost two children and her first love—but she remained deeply aggrieved that she had never been allowed to have a formal education. Her mother, Lady Redesdale, reactionary even for her day, believed girls did not need school. To the end of her life, Decca earnestly made lists of books she thought she should have read and quizzed friends about what they were reading; Dinky says that when she was a child, her mother used to sail in to confront teachers and school administrators but later confessed she was terrified of them. The only time Dinky remembers her mother being seriously angry with her was when she dropped out of Sarah Lawrence. Took Decca three days to get over it.

One of the best stories is about the time Decca was invited to become a distinguished professor at San Jose State University. She was deeply thrilled, but the position required her to take a loyalty oath. She refused to give the school her fingerprints, providing toe prints instead. A great and glorious uproar ensued, and alas, it ended with her becoming, as she put it, "an extinguished professor." She learned recently that plans were afoot at the University of California, Berkeley, to raise money for a chair in her name in investigative journalism, "I'm to be a chair, Bobby," she marveled. "A chair."

In her long life as a journalist-activist—interviewing prisoners, scouring the fringes of Oakland for her husband's labor and civil-rights cases, going to Mississippi, confronting police chiefs, taking on the medical profession—she never lost the sense that it was all a grand adventure. Shortly before her death, she said, "Well, I had a good run, didn't I?"

The New York Times Book Review
August 25, 1996

A Trumpet Calling to
the Best in Us

The irony of Ralph Yarborough's death coming so quickly after Barbara Jordan's escaped no one. There went 60 percent of the courage, 50 percent of the compassion, and 50 percent of the intellect in Texas politics in just a few days. Truly we are bereaved.

Yarborough the Lion-Hearted, dead at ninety-two, at least had his full measure of years. And to what splendid use he put them. If you look back through "Raff" Yarborough's years with the full benefit of historical perspective, his integrity and courage are astounding. He was simply right, so early, so often, and with such courage.

Politically, he was a very lonely man. From his early days in the attorney general's office in the 1930s (when he fought for the dedication of the oil royalties from our public lands for the public schools) to the 1960s (when he was the only Southern senator to vote for the Civil Rights Act in 1964 and one of the very first to oppose the war in Vietnam), Yarborough often fought alone.

I cannot begin to encompass his entire political career, so I will only try to give you a sense of him, of how he worked and spoke and was, and of his passion for justice. He was pure East Texas populist but with a populism informed by vast learning. His 1927 grade-point average at the University of Texas at Austin's law school is the stuff of legend and remains unsurpassed today. He was a judge at thirty-three. He read so widely that he knew whole civilizations the way most of us know the neighborhoods in our town. He had not an ounce of arrogance to him; he dedicated his life to "plain folks."

Picture a campaign summer in the 1950s, say, in East Texas, Raff Yarborough on the back of a flatbed truck with a C&W band in tow. Yarborough on a tear, explaining to plain folks in plain words the right and the wrong of Jim Crow, of McCarthyism, of communism, of Hispanic field workers, of the oil companies ripping off Texas, of the gutless politicians who let it happen. Any politicians who get an applause line today will stop and enjoy the clapping. Not Yarborough. Folks would start clapping, and he'd get off an even better line over the applause. And then another. And then another. And then another, until the people were on their feet cheering, and then he'd top them all.

We had retail politics in those days, and going out to hear Raff Yarborough talk was high entertainment; everybody would bring Granny and the kids and a blanket and a picnic and settle down to hear him. It was better than the Chautauqua. No one makes speeches that long nowadays; Yarborough never did learn to shorten them for the television age. The Bible and Homer, Sam Houston and Marcus Aurelius, James Madison and Bob Wills, all in one speech. And always with that drumbeat for justice, simple justice, because he believed so passionately that's what this country is about.

In those days, children, there were no Republicans in Texas. Young people used to call home from college to report to their parents they'd actually met one. We had only two flavors of Democrats. The Democratic Establishment was Lyndon B. Johnson, who whored for the oil companies back then; Allan Shivers, who was a dreadful man; and John Connally, who served them both. Yarborough fought them all, and against a stacked deck to boot. The party had the unit rule and all other manner of rules that could be used to suppress dissident opinion. This led to famous walkouts and shutouts at state conventions.

The means used to defeat and suppress Yarborough, who was anathema to the Establishment, were legion. One of the most famous was *The Port Arthur Story,* a "documentary" film used to defeat Yarborough in his 1954 gubernatorial race. It was the first half-hour political ad ever run on statewide television, and it began with a camera panning the deserted streets of downtown Port Arthur.

"This," said the announcer, "is what happens when organized labor comes to your city." The retail clerks in Port Arthur were attempting to unionize at the time, but the deserted streets were not the consequence of fearsome organized labor; they were deserted because they were filmed at 5:30 A.M.

Raff used to claim that the Establishment had spent "meel-yons and meel-yons of dollars" to defeat him, and so they did. Lloyd Bentsen finally beat him in the 1970 primary by spending the then-unimaginable sum of $6 million. In a Yarborough campaign, it was always the people against the money, and as money came to weigh more and more in our politics, voices like Raff's were squeezed out of office. But never silenced. That great trumpet sounded again and again, calling to the best in us, for freedom, for justice, for peace.

Fort Worth Star-Telegram
January 30, 1996

The Good Mother Who Put
a Shoe in the Icebox

My mother died the other day. Margaret Milne Ivins was a gay and gracious lady, and also one of the kindest people I've ever known. In eighty-four years of living, she never mastered the more practical aspects of life—I believe the correct clinical term is "seriously ditzy"—but she was nobody's fool.

She was shrewd about people and fond of fun, and at her best she could charm the birds from the trees. She was also lazy, a horrible housekeeper, somewhat depressive, and addicted to soap operas, but hey, nobody's perfect.

She believed in Education, Good Manners, and Kindness to Everyone. Actually, I believe she thought Good Manners and Kindness to Everyone were the same thing; they probably are. Her Everyone included the most hilarious cast of characters; among my mother's dear friends were the people behind the counter at the dry cleaner's, bank tellers, grocery-store clerks, and the guys at the gas station. My father used to claim that the house would look better if she would stop treating the maid like a sorority sister, but she never did.

As you can gather, she led a somewhat privileged life. Her father was well-to-do; she attended private schools, and after her graduation from Smith College (Class of '34), she went on a yearlong tour of Europe with two chums. That was in the days when one traveled on ships with steamer trunks so one could dress for dinner.

But there are different kinds of deprivation. My mother's mother died in a flu epidemic in the days before penicillin, when Mom was sixteen. I don't think she ever recovered from that sense of abandonment. She tried to comfort her grieving father and to mother her two much younger siblings, but it was too much for her. She later recalled that "my life was saved" by a caring teacher at the Roycemore School for Girls in Evanston, Illinois, who noticed that Miss Milne kept falling asleep in class from exhaustion. The teacher confronted my grandfather about it, and Mom was sent to boarding school at Walnut Hill in Massachusetts.

She went on to Smith, where her mother had gone before her and I went in my turn. (I know—this is so WASP, I'm about to urp myself.) In the midst of the Depression my grandfather couldn't afford a third year at Smith, so she spent her junior year, she always said, as "a broad in Montana," where she lived with her cousins, pledged Kappa Kappa Gamma in Missoula—later my sister's sorority—and had far too much fun. She was one of the first women ever to graduate from Smith with a degree in psychology, then considered rather a suspect field.

The evidence of that degree in her later life came in the form of her shrewd and unsparing readings of character and human relationships, including her own. She also raised her children with an unusual degree of liberality for that era; she never spanked any of us and cared not a jot for the reservations of her Texas neighbors about this college-educated Yankee lady.

Perhaps this is egocentric of me, but I think that being a mother was the central role of my mom's life. She once told me—the only one of her children never to give her a grandchild—that to the extent (in John Donne's phrase) that no man is an island, the closest relationship one can ever have with another human being on this earth is mother/child.

Not that she regarded us as an unmitigated blessing. Like all moms, she could be a royal pain in the rear. And although she was our greatest cheerleader, she certainly took seriously her motherly duty to keep any of us from getting a swelled head.

I once had a book on the bestseller list for six months and pointed this out to her, inviting maternal approval. She said, "Yes, but I see you've slipped to last on the list." Now, that's graduate-level mothering.

I once opened our family refrigerator to find a shoe and an alarm clock inside. No wonder she could never find anything. She, of course, always claimed that we made up these stories, but as my sibs will testify, she frequently mixed up our names and, when truly flustered, would address us by the dog's name.

My mother was one of those women who are just gooey about babies. She always insisted that they smell good. As any fool knows, they frequently don't, but in my mother's ideal world, no one would ever mention bodily functions. In her endless and futile effort to turn me into a lady, she once advised my ten-year-old self that the proper response to having a horse step on your foot is, "Oh, fudge!" My mother doted shamelessly on her grandchildren and lived just long enough to meet the first great-grand and pronounce him quite the most wonderful baby there ever was.

Mother was the most teasable person I ever knew, and my brother Andy could get her to laughing so hard at her own foibles that tears would run down her cheeks. When Sara and I joined in, she would denounce us as "dreadful children, perfectly dreadful children." As my cousin Johnny said, "How can you not love a woman who loves Goo-Goo Clusters?"

My mother not only read but also traveled a great deal in her later years, usually with Smith College or Smithsonian Institution groups, venturing to China, Japan, India, Mexico, Turkey. Her succinct analysis of the world's woes was: "Too many people—the trouble with the world is too many people." The most baby-loving woman I ever knew was a great supporter of birth control and abortion rights. She had a bumper sticker on her car that said, PRO-FAMILY, PRO-CHILD AND PRO-CHOICE.

Politically, she was a lifelong Republican. She used to specify "Taft Republican" until people forgot who Taft was; then she claimed "liberal Republican" and refused to admit that it was an oxymoron. She loathed Richard Nixon on the unimpeachable grounds that he was "not a nice man."

Just a few months ago her beloved Scots terrier died. She explained how much she missed him by saying: "He had such excellent political judgment. We would watch the news together, and I would say: 'Duffie, there's that horrid Mr. Gingrich again. Isn't he an awful person?' And Duffie would thump his tail on the floor in agreement. He was a terribly smart dog."

What, peculiar? My mom?

A friend of mine claims that my mother must have been the model for the Helen Hokinson cartoons in *The New Yorker.* O.K., that was her type, but she was as shrewd as she was ditzy. It was like living with a combination of Sigmund Freud and Gracie Allen. Looking on the bright side, at least we'll never have to eat turnip fluff again.

When it came to the "memorials preferred" on the obit form, we put in her favorite causes, but if you truly wanted to memorialize my mother, you would eat a piece of fudge today, hug someone you love, and be blindingly pleasant to a total stranger.

Fort Worth Star-Telegram
January 9, 1997

ABOUT THE AUTHOR

MOLLY IVINS is a nationally syndicated columnist who writes for the *Fort Worth Star-Telegram.* She has written for national newspapers and magazines, including *The New York Times, Time,* and *Newsweek.* She lives in Austin, Texas.

ABOUT THE TYPE

This book was set in Garamond, a typeface designed by the French printer Jean Jannon. It is styled after Garamond's original models. The face is dignified, and is light but without fragile lines. The Italic is modeled after a font of Granjon, which was probably cut in the middle of the sixteenth century.